AI in Healthcare: The Doctor Will Code You Now

GoodMan, Volume 1

Patrick Mukosha

Published by Patrick Mukosha, 2025.

Also by Patrick Mukosha

GoodMan
Resilient Strategies: Thriving in Harsh Business Conditions
Strategic Entrepreneurship: Navigating The Path To Success
Decisive Power: Navigating How to Make Toughest Decisions
"Reigning the Boardroom: A Trailblazing Guide to Corporate Governance Success"
Fortifying Digital Fortress: A Comprehensive Guide to Information Systems Security
"Unleashing the Power of Inclusive Innovation: Transforming the World for All"
"Exploring Computer Systems: From Fundamentals to Advanced Concepts"
"Computer Viruses Unveiled: Types, Trends and Mitigation Strategies"
"The Pinnacle of Success: Unveiling the World's 20 Most Successful Brands in 2023"
"Mastering Relational Databases: From Fundamentals to Advanced Concepts"
"Navigating Change: A Comprehensive Guide to Change Management"
"Information Systems Unraveled: Exploring the Core Concepts"
"Careers in Information Technology: Network Engineer"

“Careers in Information Technology: Network and Systems Administrator”
“Careers in Information Technology: Database Administrator”
"Careers in Information Technology: Cybersecurity Analyst"
“Careers in Information Technology: Cloud Security Specialist”
"Careers in Information Technology: Blockchain Developer"
"Careers in Information Technology: DevOps Engineer"
"Careers in Information Technology: Quality Assurance Analyst"
"Careers in Information Technology: Machine Learning Engineer"
"Careers in Information Technology: Artificial Intelligence (AI) Engineer"
"Careers in Information Technology: Internet of Things (IoT) Developer"
"Careers in Information Technology: AR/VR Developer"
“Careers in Information Technology: IoT Embedded Systems Designer”
“Careers in Information Technology: Artificial Intelligence (AI) Robotics Engineer”
“Careers in Information Technology: IoT Solutions Engineer”
“Careers in Information Technology: Data Scientist”
"Careers in Information Technology: Computer Vision Engineer"
"The Sociology of Information Technology"
“Smart Cities: The Technology Transforming Urban Living”
"The Future of Connectivity: Unleashing the Power of 5G and Beyond"
" Cybersecurity 2030 - Strategies for a Secure Digital Future"
The AI-Human Merger: Becoming Super-Intelligent Beings
AI Unleashed: The Future of Artificial Intelligence and Human Evolution
The Digital Prophet: Predicting the Next Decade of Disruption
AI in Agriculture: Farming the Future
AI in Education: Teaching the Machines to Teach

Deep Signal: AI and IoT Unlocking Underground Mining Communication
AI in Energy: Powering the Smart Grid
The Great Unlearning: How Artificial Intelligence Is Rewriting the Value of a Degree
AI in Law: Justice by Algorithm
AI in Healthcare: The Doctor Will Code You Now

Table of Contents

AI in Healthcare:
The Doctor Will Code You Now

Revolutionizing Diagnostics, Patient Care, Drug Discovery, and Medical Imaging.

Copyright Notice

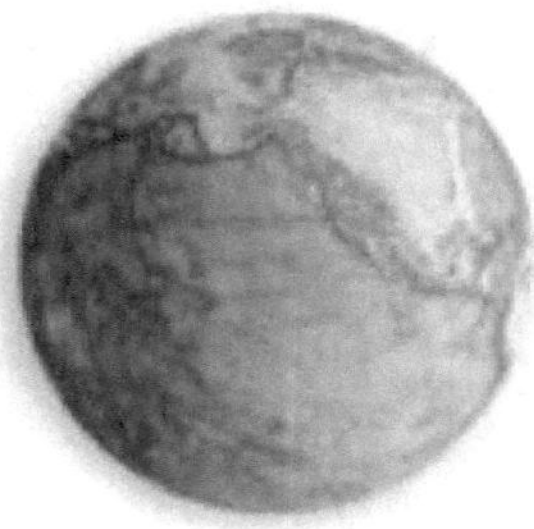

First Published: November, 2025

Publisher: Dr. Patrick Mukosha

Trademarks

Warning and Disclaimer

Author: Dr. Patrick Mukosha

Abstract

Artificial intelligence is at the heart of the biggest change in healthcare history. Algorithms that diagnose earlier, monitor continuously, scan more accurately, and accelerate drug discovery at previously unheard-of speeds can now support what once required years of knowledge, lengthy hours of analysis, and vast teams of professionals.

In order to provide readers a clear and realistic understanding of this change, I wrote ***AI in Healthcare:*** *The Doctor Will Code You Now.*

This book aims to demonstrate how artificial intelligence (AI) is becoming a vital partner in contemporary medicine, not to replace physicians. The future of healthcare is now being developed, from AI-designed medicines to intelligent patient care and predictive diagnostics.

My goal is straightforward: *to provide a useful, forward-thinking guide to the technology that will characterize the next wave of healthcare, all the while addressing the human, safety, and ethical issues that must direct this transformation.*

You will learn:

- How AI improves clinical accuracy and outperforms conventional diagnostics in this ground-breaking book.
- How proactive, ongoing healthcare is being transformed by clever patient monitoring.
- How precision dosage that is customized for each patient is made possible by AI-driven medication development, which is speeding up treatments.
- How automation, deep learning, and previously unheard-of insight are revolutionizing medical imaging.

Future clinics will continue to rely on clinical judgment and human compassion. However, data, algorithms, and intelligent systems that improve each stage of care will also power it.

Welcome to a time where the machine learns, the doctor codes, and they all work together to heal more intelligently.

Chapter 1: Introduction - The Rise of the AI Doctor

Overview of AI's Promise and Threats in Modern Healthcare

Artificial intelligence is now the newest member of the medical team, not just a futuristic concept discussed in research labs. AI-powered systems are increasingly used in radiology suites, operating rooms, oncology wards, emergency rooms, and other settings to diagnose illnesses, suggest treatments, forecast patient decline, and even help with difficult surgeries. The "AI Doctor" has emerged to improve, supplement, and occasionally question the fundamental principles of medical practice rather than to replace human clinicians.

This chapter provides an *overview of the rapidly developing field of AI-driven healthcare, looking at both its enormous potential and the real risks it presents*. We examine how AI is changing medical research, diagnostics, patient care, ethics, and the doctor-patient relationship through case studies, real-world examples, and forward-looking ideas.

1.1. The Emergence of Intelligent Medical Machines

Artificial intelligence (AI) started to change healthcare from human-driven intuition to data-driven precision with the advent of machine-intelligent medicine. Early uses concentrated on automating repetitive processes such as predictive risk assessment, patient record maintenance, and medical imaging analysis. *Computers can now identify patterns in complicated datasets that are frequently invisible to humans thanks to machine learning algorithms, which enables quicker, more precise diagnoses and individualized treatment regimens.*

AI was also included into robotic-assisted surgery, genomics, and drug development during this time, laying the groundwork for a future in which AI serves as a cooperative "*Clinical Partner*" rather than merely a tool. It generated important ethical and legal concerns regarding responsibility, patient privacy, and the role of human judgment in medical decision-making, even while it promised previously unheard-of efficiency and precision.

For instance, AI systems like Google's DeepMind and IBM Watson Health showed early effectiveness in evaluating imaging data and forecasting patient decline, demonstrating how robots may supplement—and occasionally even surpass—conventional clinical methods.

For many years, digital patient records and simple decision-support tools were the main use of computing in medicine. These days, medicine has entered a new era thanks to robotic intelligence, deep neural networks, generative AI models, and reinforcement learning systems.

These days, machines are able to:

- *Identify cancer before radiologists do.*
- *Foresee heart failure before symptoms manifest.*

- *Provide sub-millimetre precision to surgeons.*
- *In just a few minutes, analyse intricate genomic data.*
- *Automate administrative duties that used to take up 40% of a clinician's time.*

AI is more than a tool. It is evolving into a clinical partner.

For instance: An Additional Set of Eyes in Radiology

A big multi-centre radiology research conducted in 2023 found that AI-assisted mammography reduced false positives by 25% while increasing breast cancer detection by 20%. Radiologists started referring to the system as a "tireless second reader" since it consistently provided objective analysis even during night shifts that were prone to tiredness.

This change is an example of how AI is complementing medical professionals rather than taking their place.

1.2. The Reasons AI in Healthcare Is Now Unavoidable

The combination of excessive data, growing patient expectations, and the constraints of conventional medical procedures made AI in healthcare inevitable. No human doctor can adequately interpret the vast volumes of data generated by modern medicine in real time, from genomic sequences and wearable technology to Electronic Health Records (EHRs) and medical imaging. AI is essential for prompt, correct decision-making because of its quick processing and interpretation of this data.

Furthermore, there was a need for scalable, accurate, and affordable solutions due to the growing complexity of patients, aging populations, and the worldwide scarcity of medical experts. *AI improves results while lowering errors and inefficiencies by providing predictive analytics for early disease detection, individualized treatment strategies, and ongoing monitoring.*

As an illustration, during the COVID-19 pandemic, AI-powered models anticipated the spread of the disease, optimized hospital resource allocation, and expedited drug repurposing efforts—showing that intelligent, automated systems are essential to meeting today's healthcare concerns.

Three factors are coming together to propel the development of AI:

1. **Data Explosion:** Massive datasets are produced by modern healthcare, including genomic sequencing, MRI scans, wearable sensor data, and EHR notes. AI thrives on this data since it is too big for humans to handle.

2. **Clinical Pressures:** Hospital treatment is becoming more complex, patient loads are increasing, and there is a

persistent shortage of specialists. AI acts as a multiplier of clinical competence, bridging the gap.

3. **Advances in Computing:** Complex medical algorithms can now operate in real-time, even on portable devices, thanks to advancements in GPUs, cloud computing, and massive language models.

1.3. Case Study: How AI Saved a Life in an Emergency Room

A middle-aged patient with acute chest discomfort and dyspnoea showed up at a crowded urban emergency room. An AI-powered triage system analysing real-time vital signs, medical history, and imaging data found subtle patterns suggestive of a rare but potentially fatal Aortic Dissection—*a condition frequently overlooked by human clinicians due to its resemblance to common heart attacks*—while preliminary testing indicated a routine cardiac issue.

The medical staff was promptly notified by the AI, which highlighted the serious risk and recommended fast diagnostic imaging. Following this advice, medical professionals performed emergency surgery and verified the diagnosis. Follow-up showed that the dissection might have been lethal in the absence of the AI intervention, but the patient lived.

Key Takeaways:

- Machine intelligence can serve as a quick, second-opinion system, assisting human decision-making in life-or-death situations;
- AI integration in emergency care improves speed and accuracy, potentially saving countless lives;
- AI excels at identifying hidden patterns and rare conditions that can be overlooked in high-pressure settings.

Case: The Quiet Heart Attack

A 54-year-old guy with modest chest pain entered an emergency room in Los Angeles. His EKG looked normal. He might have been released under traditional screening.

However, the hospital had implemented an AI-powered EKG analysis model that had been trained on millions of cardiac rhythms.

The AI identified "high-risk: possible anterior myocardial infarction," which prompted an emergency angiography and troponin test right away.

Result: Within 40 minutes, a completely clogged artery was found and treated. Physicians gave the AI system credit for spotting the subtle pattern that was missed by the human eye.

This story highlights how machine intelligence may save lives in front-line healthcare.

1.4. The AI Doctor's Promise

The "AI Doctor" portrays a future in which AI is an active collaborator in healthcare delivery rather than only a tool. It has the potential to provide human therapists with unmatched data processing, pattern identification, and predictive insights. *AI is capable of quickly analysing enormous information, ranging from genetics and wearable technology to electronic health records and medical imaging, allowing for highly customized diagnoses and treatment regimens for every patient.*

Beyond diagnosis, AI might transform preventative care, provide real-time monitoring of chronic illnesses, and streamline hospital operations to cut down on errors, delays, and expenses. It can bridge gaps in human expertise and time restrictions by helping with drug discovery, simulating treatment outcomes, and even forecasting epidemics before they worsen.

As an illustration, AI-powered virtual assistants are already serving as diligent clinical collaborators by assisting doctors with patient triage, treatment protocol recommendations, and the identification of high-risk cases. The AI Doctor promises a quicker, smarter, and more accurate healthcare system while freeing up human physicians to concentrate on complicated decision-making, empathy, and moral judgment that computers cannot match.

AI has the potential to revolutionize almost every aspect of healthcare.

1.4.1. **Diagnostics: Superhuman Identification of Patterns**

AI's capacity to identify patterns in medical data at a level that frequently exceeds human competence is one of its most revolutionary contributions to healthcare. *AI systems can evaluate complicated datasets, like imaging scans, lab findings, and genomic sequences, using machine learning and deep learning algorithms to find minor abnormalities that even the most skilled medical professionals would miss.*

Every minute counts when it comes to the early diagnosis of diseases like cancer, neurological problems, and uncommon genetic conditions, which is accelerated by this "superhuman pattern recognition." Additionally, AI can continuously learn from new cases, increasing its accuracy and decreasing diagnostic errors over time.

Example: AI algorithms in radiology have shown that they can detect early-stage lung cancer nodules in CT scans more accurately than radiologists, allowing for earlier intervention and greatly enhancing patient outcomes. AI is quite good at spotting minute irregularities that are not obvious to the human eye.

For instance:

- **Ophthalmology:** Using a retinal photo taken in a remote clinic, AI models can identify diabetic retinopathy with 96% accuracy.
- **Dermatology:** The precision with which smartphone apps categorize skin lesions is now on par with that of board-certified dermatologists.
- **Pathology:** Analysis of digital slides AI finds micro-metastases that pathologists could miss after a long day.

AI never grows weary. It is not forgetful. There is no cognitive bias in it.

1.4.2. **Predictive Analytics: Medication Prior to Symptoms**

By enabling medical professionals to foresee illness before it appears, predictive analytics in healthcare can move medicine from reactive to proactive treatment. Artificial intelligence algorithms can detect early warning signs and trends that anticipate the start of illnesses like diabetes, heart disease, or sepsis by evaluating large datasets, including patient histories, test findings, genetics, lifestyle factors, and even wearable device data.

This pre-emptive strategy lowers complications, hospital stays, and medical expenses by enabling actions to take place before symptoms manifest. By identifying high-risk populations and improving preventive measures, predictive analytics also aids in population health management.

Healthcare is becoming proactive instead than reactive thanks to AI.

Example: Sepsis Prediction Systems

More people die from sepsis worldwide than from all malignancies put together. Up to six hours before doctors suspect sepsis, predictive AI models used in intensive care units are now able to identify early indicators, such as variations in oxygen saturation, heart rate variability, and subtle lab abnormalities.

AI models in intensive care units can predict sepsis hours before clinical symptoms manifest, providing medical professionals with vital time to deliver life-saving therapy.

Predictive algorithms can also identify individuals who are at a high risk of heart attacks or strokes, allowing for early lifestyle changes or preventative treatments.

In a few of hospitals, early intervention has reduced mortality rates by 20–40%.

1.4.3. Precision Medicine: Customizing Care for Each Patient

By using AI to customize healthcare based on a patient's genetics, environment, lifestyle, and medical history, precision medicine goes beyond the "one-size-fits-all" approach. In order to determine which treatments are most likely to be successful for a particular patient, AI algorithms may evaluate intricate genomic data, biomarkers, and treatment responses, enhancing results while reducing side effects.

In oncology, unusual genetic abnormalities, and the management of chronic diseases, where patient responses to conventional treatments differ greatly, this approach is especially revolutionary. By forecasting how people will react to experimental treatments, AI also speeds up the drug discovery process and allows for more individualized care.

For instance, AI may examine a patient's tumour genome and match it with treatments that target particular mutations, significantly raising the chance of remission and minimizing needless exposure to useless medications.

AI analyses genomic profiles, expedites medication discovery, and optimizes treatment regimens.

Case Study: Uncommon Genetic Illness Diagnosis

An unexplained developmental problem affected a youngster in the United Kingdom. An AI-assisted genomic study reduced the number of potential mutations from 25,000 to just three plausible culprits after years of inconclusive testing.

A treatment plan was created in a matter of weeks, drastically altering the child's course.

1.4.4. **Efficiency and Automation: Relieving Physicians of the "Digital Clerical Burden"**

Automating repetitive, time-consuming chores that take up clinicians' attention—often referred to as the "digital clerical burden"—is a major promise of AI in healthcare. Intelligent systems may now do tasks like data input, charting, appointment scheduling, insurance documentation, and even initial diagnostic evaluations.

AI frees up doctors to concentrate on what they do best—direct patient care, complicated decision-making, and empathetic interaction—by relieving them of these administrative responsibilities. Additionally, automation speeds up workflow and lowers errors related to human record-keeping, increasing hospital productivity and patient throughput.

AI-powered documentation assistants, for instance, can automatically update electronic health records, transcribe and summarize notes, listen to doctor-patient consultations in real time, and identify any problems for review. In the end, this improves patient safety by saving hours every day and guaranteeing more accurate, consistent records.

These days, AI assistants can:

- Produce clinical notes from voice conversations.
- Provide a summary of the lab findings.
- Take care of medical coding.

Plan follow-up appointments with patients.

Clinicians may resume providing actual patient care, which is what they were trained for, by saving three to five hours every day.

1.5. The Dangers: When the AI Physician Makes a Mistake

The AI Doctor has a lot of promise, but if it's used improperly or overused, there are serious concerns. *AI systems may make mistakes in uncommon or unusual situations, misinterpret intricate medical details, or acquire biases from faulty datasets.* AI lacks ethical judgment and sensibility, unlike human physicians, which can result in risky mistakes if results are seen as perfect.

Another issue is cybersecurity. Due to their reliance on enormous volumes of private patient data, medical AI systems are prime candidates for ransomware, hacking, and data manipulation. In therapeutic contexts, even minor algorithmic mistakes or software bugs might have potentially fatal outcomes.

Furthermore, an excessive reliance on AI may eventually deteriorate doctors' abilities, making it harder for them to make crucial choices when technology malfunctions. Since regulatory frameworks are still developing, it might be difficult to determine who is responsible for AI-driven mistakes, which complicates ethical and legal obligations.

As an illustration of how relying on flawed algorithms can directly affect patients, it was discovered in 2019 that an AI system used to forecast patient deterioration in hospitals persistently underestimated risk for specific ethnic groups due to biased training data.

AI has enormous potential, but it also poses real hazards that need to be addressed.

1.5.1. **Bias: Inheriting Inequality in Algorithms**

Although artificial intelligence is sometimes promoted as impartial, objective, and data-driven, in practice, AI systems may inherit the same disparities found in the communities that create them. This becomes a subtle and severe menace in the healthcare industry: algorithms trained on biased data may inadvertently favour some populations and disadvantage others, increasing the disparity in treatment outcomes.

a. Algorithmic Bias's Origin

AI bias is a direct result of historical, social, and structural injustices ingrained in the data; it does not just happen. AI gains knowledge from:

- **Biased Datasets:** The AI model will not generalize well to different demographics if clinical datasets mostly include data from one group (such as Western, urban, or insured patients).
- **Human Judgments:** Previous medical judgments, some of which were impacted by prejudice or antiquated presumptions, serve as "ground truth" for model training.
- **Inequitable Access to Care**: The data pertaining to some groups will reflect their disadvantages if they receive poorer treatment, fewer testing, or delayed diagnosis.

To put it briefly, AI magnifies what it discovers rather than creating bias.

Actual Case: Racial Prejudice in American Hospital Algorithms

Black patients' health demands were shown to be over 50% underestimated by a prominent algorithm used by American hospitals to identify high-risk patients.

Why?

Healthcare spending was employed by the algorithm as a stand-in for the severity of the sickness. Black patients have historically received less care, which has led to lower costs; as a result, the algorithm incorrectly determined that they were healthier.

This resulted in the exclusion of thousands of vulnerable patients from essential support programs.

a. The Practice of Healthcare Bias

Many medical AI applications are susceptible to subtle bias:

- AI for dermatological diagnostic imaging that struggles with darker skin tones.
- Why Black and brown patients' oxygen levels are overestimated by pulse oximeters, which are now often employed in AI-driven patient monitoring.
- Chatbots and triage AI that may give priority to symptoms "commonly reported" by some groups while ignoring the ways in which other populations manifest sickness.
- Drug response predictors that were trained on a lack of genetic variation put entire communities at risk for harmful responses or incorrect diagnoses.

a. Why This Matters

Bias in healthcare is more than just a software flaw; it can also mean:

- Delays in cancer diagnosis and unequal access to cardiac care;
- Inaccurate medication dosage;
- Underestimation of pain;

- Preventable fatalities.

AI has the potential to save lives, but if it is developed improperly, it can also covertly maintain widespread inequalities.

a. Safeguarding Patients: How to Limit AI Prejudice

To prevent AI from inheriting injustice, healthcare institutions can take the following actions:

- **Employ a variety of international datasets:** Incorporate significant differences in geography, age, gender, ethnicity, and socioeconomic status.
- **Conduct Audits Of Bias**: Analyse algorithm performance not just overall accuracy but also across subgroups.
- **Development Transparency**: Clearly state datasets, procedures, and system constraints.
- **Control and Keep an Eye on Actual Performance**: After deployment, algorithms should be regularly assessed, not only during testing.
- **Human Oversight**: AI should complement clinical judgment rather than take its place.

Health disparities may get worse if AI algorithms are trained on skewed data.

Example: Biased Insurance Risk Model

In the past, a popular insurance algorithm gave preference to healthy white patients for more care over Black patients with more serious illnesses. This was due to the fact that Black areas had historically had lower spending, which the model was trained on.

This example demonstrates how, if not properly audited, AI might exacerbate social injustices.

1.5.2. Overreliance: When Physicians Rely More on AI Than Their Own Discretion

Over-reliance is a new and subtle risk that has surfaced as AI grows in capability and integration into clinical operations. At this point, medical personnel start to rely more on recommendations from AI than on their own clinical judgment, even if the AI is incorrect.

It is simple to see how clinicians could submit to AI in a time when algorithms seem to be flawless and robots perform better than experts in some diagnostic tasks. However, this naive optimism may have disastrous consequences.

1. The Reasons Behind Overreliance

Although doctors are taught to critically examine, assess evidence, and challenge presumptions, AI is particularly alluring for a number of reasons:

- **Perceived Objectivity**: AI is perceived as "scientific," a result of intricate mathematics rather than human frailty.
- **Time Constraints**: Doctors who are overworked might accept AI results in order to make choices more quickly.
- **Automation Bias**: People have a tendency to believe that automated systems are more accurate.
- **Institutional Pressure**: AI-driven procedures that seem more economical or efficient may be promoted by hospitals.

- **Fear of Being Mistaken**: Many medical professionals are reluctant to question an AI system that promises 98% accuracy.

However, clinical intuition, experiential knowledge, and contextual understanding—qualities that no machine completely possesses—can be superseded by the appearance of perfection.

1. **Case Study: The Inaccurate Stroke Diagnosis**

An AI triage tool was employed in a European emergency room in 2024 to categorize patients according to the severity of their symptoms. The AI classified a middle-aged patient exhibiting mild neurological symptoms, such as dizziness and slurred speech, as "non-urgent."

When the attending nurse sensed something wasn't quite right, she thought about overriding the AI but eventually decided to trust it. Before being checked, the patient had to wait more than three hours.

He had experienced a minor ischemic stroke.

Permanent speech impairment was the outcome of the delay.

This example highlights the risk: the AI was not malevolent; rather, it lacked the contextual complexity that a human physician would naturally pick up on.

However, human judgment was overshadowed by the Trust-in-AI effect.

1. **The Signs of Overreliance in Healthcare**

Overreliance can appear in a variety of areas:

- **Radiology:** Physicians accept AI annotations without reassessing scans.
- **Diagnostics:** AI makes a new diagnosis, therefore it overrides "gut feeling."
- **Prescribing**: Selecting AI-recommended medication combinations even when adverse effects defy professional judgment.
- **Triage:** Using AI risk rankings to decide who needs emergency care.
- **Surgery:** Relying on robotic suggestions for incision locations or methods without checking them.

AI turns from a tool into a crutch in every circumstance.

1. **Blind Trust's Dangers**

Generally, there are two types of AI errors:

- **Systematic Errors:** Repeated mistakes on a large scale (e.g., consistently misclassifying specific symptoms).
- **Contextual Blind Spots**: Situations in which patient-specific information is not included in the training set of the model. When medical professionals rely too much on AI, these mistakes spread swiftly and covertly, frequently impacting thousands of people before being discovered.

Misdiagnosis and delayed treatment, improper medication, unneeded operations, deadly oversights, and a decline in professional expertise and intuition are some of the consequences.

The tragedy lies not in AI's errors but rather in humans ceasing to double-check.

1. **Establishing a Positive Human-AI Collaboration**

Rejecting AI is not the answer; balanced use is:

- AI should support medical professionals, not take their place.
- AI recommendations must be verified by protocols.
- AI results ought to be regarded as a second opinion rather than a verdict.
- To comprehend the limitations of AI, clinicians must receive training.
- Rather than using AI mindlessly, hospitals should promote a culture of inquiry.

AI and physicians by themselves are not the most potent healthcare systems.

In this relationship, humans contribute context, wisdom, and empathy while machines supply speed and scalability.

Confidence scores from AI might be alluring.

Example: A Misclassification Incident in Radiology

A benign lesion was mistakenly classified as "high probability cancer" in 2024 by a lung-nodule algorithm.

A needless biopsy resulted from the clinician's faith in the machine.

The hospital subsequently found that the inaccuracy was caused by a problem with the training dataset's data labelling.

Human supervision is still essential.

1.5.3. Cybersecurity Risks: The Situation of the Hacked Hospital

Hospitals are becoming more appealing targets for cybercriminals as they get smarter, more automated, and equipped with AI-driven technologies. An AI-powered scanner, automated medication dispensers, smart infusion pumps, remote monitoring systems, electronic records, cloud platforms, and even surgical robots are just a few of the many interconnected technologies that make up a modern hospital.

Attacks on this digital economy have repercussions that go beyond money.

Cybersecurity lapses in the medical field cost lives.

1. The Reasons AI-Powered Hospitals Are Top Priorities

Hospitals have never had to defend against new assault surfaces brought about by AI. Both state-sponsored hacking groups and cybercriminals are aware of this.

Among the main weaknesses are:

- AI decision-making systems that are susceptible to manipulation to provide erroneous results.
- IoT-connected medical equipment that don't have robust

security measures.
- Cloud-based electronic health records (EHRs) are a prime target for identity theft.
- Automated processes that, in the event of a breach, collapse.
- Antiquated hospital IT systems that are vulnerable to contemporary cyberattacks.

Hospitals cannot simply "shut down" during an assault, unlike banks or IT businesses, which would exacerbate the effects.

1. Case Study: The Hospital's Dark Night

Imagine the following situation, which is based on actual events that have actually happened all across the world:

A large urban hospital's emergency room abruptly becomes silent at 2:13 AM.

The screens for triage freeze. The patient monitoring system driven by AI disconnects. Error codes appear on ventilators. Medication is no longer dispensed by the robotic pharmacy. CT scanners won't turn on.

Every monitor displays the following message: *"Your network has been encrypted."* **Restore access by paying $5 million.**

Physicians rush to transition to manual procedures.

In the middle of a procedure, surgeons stop using robotic systems.

Paper charts are used again by nurses.

For thirty-two critically ill patients, the ICU loses real-time monitoring.

Within hours:

- Two stroke patients miss the life-saving "golden hour" window for clot-busting therapy;
- The neonatal ward loses temperature regulation control, necessitating emergency evacuations;
- A ransomware group releases partial patient records on the dark web;
- One patient dies from a preventable cardiac arrest because the AI-alert system never triggered.

Six days passed during the attack.

Restoring full functionality took two months.

The harm to one's reputation persisted for years.

This is not science fiction; comparable incidents have occurred in South Africa, Germany, the United States, and Ireland. Cyberattacks damaged hospitals and put patients in danger in each instance.

1.5.4. **How AI Systems Are Used by Hackers**

Cybercriminals take use of many vulnerabilities in AI-powered healthcare:

- **Data Poisoning**: Adding fictitious data to training sets to cause the AI to make risky recommendations.
- **Model Manipulation**: Changing outputs by reverse-engineering algorithms (e.g., having an AI misunderstand X-

rays).
- **Device Hijacking:** Taking over robotic surgeons, insulin pumps, infusion pumps, or pacemakers.

Attacks using ransomware encrypt hospital systems and demand money:

- **Deepfake Medical Orders:** Approving lethal medicine dosages with voice-cloned remarks or fake doctor signatures.
- **Cloud Breaches**: Remote access to AI models. In the worst situation, a hacker might inflict extensive damage without ever going inside the facility.

1.5.5. The Special Vulnerability of Healthcare

Cyber environments in the healthcare industry are vulnerable for a number of reasons:

- **Legacy Systems:** A lot of medical equipment uses out-of-date or unsupported operating systems.
- **24/7 Operations:** It is not possible to take systems offline for updates.
- **Multiple Vendors:** It's common for devices made by multiple manufacturers to be unable to securely connect.
- **Clinicians Prioritize Speed over Security:** In an emergency, staff frequently skip security procedures to save time.
- **High-Value Information**: On the illicit market, medical records are worth more than credit card numbers.

1.5.6. Constructing Cyber-Resilient Medical Facilities

A multifaceted strategy is needed to safeguard AI-enabled hospitals:

- Zero-trust security approaches that constantly authenticate each user and device.
- Medical devices with frequent updates and secure firmware that are encrypted.
- AI-powered threat detection systems that keep an eye out for irregularities in real time.
- Frequent penetration testing to find vulnerabilities before attackers do.
- Offline backup mechanisms to ensure that care is provided even in the event of a network failure.
- Cybersecurity education for medical professionals, nurses, and support personnel.
- A government rule that sets minimal cybersecurity requirements for AI used in healthcare.

1.5.7. The Important Point

AI has the potential to save lives, but it may equally be used as a weapon in the wrong hands.

A bank that has been hacked loses money.

However, a hacked hospital results in fatalities.

AI in healthcare will require both creativity and caution in the future. Even the most sophisticated medical AI becomes a ticking time bomb in the absence of robust cybersecurity.

Today, the healthcare industry is a digital battleground.

1.5.8. Situation: The Shutdown of Ransomware

An AI-targeted ransomware attack occurred in 2025 at a prominent hospital in Europe.

In the middle of a surgery, surgical robots froze.

Clinicians were locked out of the EHR system.

Insulin pumps that were automated failed.

The attack caused the hospital to go into "manual mode" for 48 hours, which led to severe patient issues and postponed surgeries.

The threat surface is significantly increased by AI systems.

1.5.9. **Loss of Human Touch: The Issue of "Cold Efficiency"**

Diagnosis, data, and decision-making are not the only aspects of healthcare. It is a deeply human service based on empathy, trust, and the therapeutic value of interpersonal relationships. However, a subtle but extremely significant threat—the loss of human touch—emerges as AI systems take over duties that have historically been completed by physicians.

We run the risk of developing a technologically sophisticated but emotionally devoid healthcare system in our pursuit of speed, automation, and efficiency.

This is the issue with cold efficiency.

1. Algorithmic Care's Ascent

Predictive analytics and pattern recognition are two areas where AI shines. It can:

- Read scans more quickly than radiologists;

- Keep a close eye on vital signs;
- Anticipate patient decline hours before people do;
- Automate medication dispensing, meal preparation, and appointment scheduling.

However, AI has one basic drawback: it is incapable of caring.

It can mimic civility, but not empathy.

It can understand symptoms, but not pain.

It can suggest therapies, but it cannot comfort anxious patients.

Something significant is lost when AI takes over the front lines of healthcare.

1. Case Study: "The Doctor Didn't Even Look at Me"

An AI-powered triage system was implemented by a big city hospital to control patient flow. Before ever meeting a nurse or physician, patients engaged with a machine.

Maria, a 67-year-old cancer survivor, complained of extreme exhaustion, light-headedness, and anxiety. Her symptoms were classified by the AI as "non-urgent," and she was sent to the regular waiting line.

She started crying when she eventually saw a doctor about three hours later: "I didn't mind waiting... No one even looked me in the eyes, which bothered me.

Although her vital signs were normal, she was in great mental suffering.

Later, she clarified that she felt invisible when speaking to a machine.

The hospital increased productivity, but at the expense of people.

1. What Patients Are Most Afraid of

Research regularly demonstrates that patients fear:

- Losing a personal connection with their providers;
- Being disregarded;
- Being misinterpreted; and
- Being treated like data rather than humans.

AI-powered systems inadvertently exacerbate these anxieties.

Patients start referring to their treatment as "clinical" or "mechanical" in the most derogatory terms.

1. The Gradual Loss of Compassion

AI poses a number of risks to empathy:

- **Less In-Person Time**: Doctors spend less time hearing patient stories when algorithms do assessments.
- **Deskilling Of Communication**: Rather than interacting directly, clinicians start depending on summaries produced by machines.
- **Protocol-Driven Interactions**: Hospitals may put efficiency measures ahead of patient care.

- **Emotional Distancing**: Doctors may miss out on chances to establish an emotional connection when AI takes care of the "listening."

Medicine gets quicker, but it grows less compassionate.

1. **The Significance of Human Touch in Healing**

Empathy is a clinical tool, not a luxury.

According to research, emotional connection can lower anxiety in patients, raise pain tolerance, boost medication adherence, improve recovery rates, lower malpractice claims, and boost patient satisfaction and trust.

There are quantifiable physiological effects from a comforting hand on the shoulder, a doctor sitting rather than standing, and a moment of listening.

AI is unable to duplicate that.

1. **Finding the Right Balance: Technology + People**

The answer is to make sure AI strengthens human connection rather than replaces it:

- **Hospitals can use:** Hybrid models, where people handle emotion and AI handles data.
- **Compassion protocols:** Human contact is required at critical junctures.
- **Emotion-aware interfaces**: Programs that notify medical professionals when a patient's emotional condition need care.
- **Training programs:** Educating healthcare professionals on how to incorporate empathy into workflows aided by AI.

- **Patient-first design**: ensuring that no patient engages with AI prior to obtaining human care.

AI should reduce the administrative load so physicians may concentrate more on human interaction rather than less.

1. The Fundamental Truth

AI speeds things up.

AI improves accuracy.

AI provides consistency.

However, only people can offer consolation, compassion, and presence.

Efficiency and compassion must not be mutually exclusive in the future of healthcare.

Developing systems that provide both is a problem and an opportunity.

1.5.10. Accountability: When AI Makes an Error, Who Is at Fault?

Take a look at this situation inspired by real life:

A woman with the typical symptoms of a pulmonary embolism shows up at the emergency department. Her risk is rated as minimal by the AI triage system, which has received plaudits for its outstanding accuracy. The attending physician deprioritizes her case because he has faith in the AI.

She passes away after collapsing some hours later.

Who is responsible?

- *The physician who trusted the AI?*
- *The medical facility that required AI-guided triage?*
- *The tech firm that developed the model?*
- *The model's training dataset?*
- *The authorities who gave their approval for its implementation?*

The line of accountability is hazy, but each party had a part to play.

1.5.11. The Four Principal Liability Models Under International Discussion

Medical boards, legislators, and ethicists are still debating who should bear accountability. Four frameworks are becoming more popular:

a. The Model of the Physician as the Final Decision-Maker.

Regardless of what AI suggests, doctors are always responsible.

Pros: Easy, safeguards patients.

Cons: Unrealistic; physicians are unable to instantly confirm each algorithmic conclusion.

a. Shared Accountability

Model Developers, hospitals, and clinicians share accountability.
Pros: Captures the intricacy of the real world.

Cons: Complicated lawsuits; difficult to implement legally.

a. Developer or Manufacturer Liability Model

AI firms are handled similarly to makers of medical devices.
Pros: Promotes more transparent and safe AI.
Cons: Businesses might decline to develop high-risk clinical AI tools.

a. Hospital-Level Responsibility System Liability Model

Hospitals using AI are solely accountable.

Pros: Hospitals are in charge of purchasing, using, and supervising.

Cons: Hospitals may limit innovation and become unduly cautious.

Globally, governments are still unsure, and the healthcare industry operates in an uncertain legal environment.

1.5.12. **The Moral Conundrum: Is a Machine to Blame?**

AI is not human. It lacks:

- Cognition,
- Moral responsibility, and
- Aim.

It is useless to blame AI per se.

However, as AI becomes more autonomous, the concept of accountability must be reconsidered.

For instance:

- *If a radiology AI misidentifies a tumour, resulting in needless surgery, was it a systemic failure or a tool malfunction?*
- *After deployment, if a self-learning model changes and loses accuracy, who is in charge of these adjustments?*
- *Is an AI's error truly a "mistake" if it is more accurate than the typical physician but nonetheless incorrect in some situations?*

We are venturing into uncharted territory.

1.5.13. Closing the Accountability Divide

Healthcare systems need to implement new measures to protect patients and foster innovation:

a. Explainability Conditions

When AI is utilized to make important decisions, its results must be justified.

a. Constant Observation

AI shouldn't only be authorized once; it should be routinely reviewed for accuracy, bias, and drift.

a. Explicit Legal Structures

Governments must enact laws that define culpability specifically for AI.

a. Definition of Roles

Formal rules need to make clear what physicians need to confirm, what hospitals need to keep an eye on, and what developers need to ensure.

a. Mandates for Human Oversight

AI must operate under human supervision; it cannot take the position of clinicians.

a. Transparency of Incidents

Similar to medication reactions or surgical mishaps, hospitals should disclose AI failures.

1.5.14. **The Fundamental Idea**

It's Time to Design Responsibility While AI presents new hazards, it also reveals an unsettling reality: accountability is not a given. It needs to be built into the system.

Clarity, transparency, and shared accountability among all stakeholders are necessary for ethical AI in healthcare.

Patients suffer and trust breaks down in the absence of this.

1.6. The New Doctor-AI Connection

The goal of artificial intelligence's emergence in healthcare is to redefine the relationship between human knowledge and machine intelligence rather than to replace doctors. Instead of doctors and AI competing, the future of medicine will be fashioned by cooperation—a partnership in which each provides skills that the other cannot match.

One of the most significant changes in medical history is represented by this developing partnership.

1.6.1. From Instruments to Teammates

Technology has historically been used as a tool, such as an MRI machine, a thermometer, and a stethoscope. But AI is not like that. It enhances a doctor's cognitive ability in addition to their physical senses. AI can:

- Already evaluate millions of patient histories in a matter of seconds,
- Find minute patterns on scans,
- Use extensive medical information to help clinical decision-making;
- Monitor patients continually without tiredness; and
- Forecast outcomes with statistical precision.

As a result, AI is now a clinical partner rather than just a "tool," able to produce real-time insights that humans could never produce on their own.

Importantly, though, AI is not a physician. It is a companion.

1.6.2. The Changing Dynamics

Complementary strengths characterize the doctor-AI relationship:

a. **The Advantages of AI**

- Recall Of Extensive,
- Intricate Medical Literature;
- Speed And Processing Capability;
- Pattern Recognition;
- Predictive analytics; consistency

a. **The doctor's strengths include**:

- Empathy And Emotional Intelligence;
- Contextual Judgment;
- Ethical Reasoning;
- Comprehension Of The Patient's Values, Fears, Culture, And Personal History; And
- Inventiveness in challenging or unfamiliar situations.

When combined, they provide a hybrid care paradigm that is significantly more effective than either one by itself.

1.6.3. An Ordinary Day in a Medical-AI Collaboration

Imagine a clinical workflow in the near future:

- **Morning Rounds**: AI identifies patients who are most likely to deteriorate overnight by displaying patterns that are invisible to humans.
- **Diagnostics:** Radiology AI uses annotated reasoning to identify worrisome lesions. The physician personally reviews the pictures, either validating or refuting the AI's recommendations.

- **Treatment Planning**: Using thousands of comparable cases, AI suggests individualized treatment plans. The doctor adjusts such recommendations based on the patient's lifestyle, tastes, financial situation, or cultural characteristics that AI is unable to comprehend.
- **Patient Communication**: The doctor, not the AI, reassures worried families, discusses plans, and delivers news.
  Clinical delivery is strengthened by AI and humanized by the physician.

1.6.4. The "Third Opinion" Model

Clinicians are increasingly using AI as a third opinion as it grows more accurate:

- **First Opinion:** The doctor's preliminary evaluation
- **Second Opinion:** When necessary, a second opinion from a human clinician
- **Third Opinion:** AI's autonomous, data-driven evaluation
  Care is safer and more dependable thanks to this triangular model's increased diagnostic accuracy and decreased cognitive bias.

1.6.5. The Doctor's New Duties

The modern physician today needs to become proficient in new skills:

- **AI Literacy:** knowing how models operate, their constraints, and when to challenge them.
- **Data Interpretation**: confirming findings produced by AI
- **Ethical Supervision:** guaranteeing equity, openness, and patient confidentiality.
- **Communication**: assisting patients in comprehending

decisions aided by AI.
- **Accountability:** maintaining final say over clinical results Physicians are becoming more strategically significant than ever, not less.

1.6.6. Patients' New Expectations

Patients anticipate the following when AI enters exam rooms:

- Explanations of how AI influenced decisions;
- Guarantee that final decisions are made by humans rather than machines;
- Openness regarding data usage;
- Defense against prejudice or an excessive dependence on automation;
- Emotional assistance that AI is unable to give.
- Now, trust is based on how successfully medical professionals use AI without sacrificing their humanity.

1.6.7. The Partnership's Promise

Faster diagnoses, fewer mistakes, tailored care, better patient outcomes, less professional burnout, and more time for meaningful doctor-patient engagement are all benefits of a well-designed and balanced doctor-AI partnership.

AI is already in the healthcare industry; the question is no longer whether it will be.

How we mold the cooperation is the true question.

1.6.8. The New Era's Fundamental Idea

AI improves medicine, but doctors are the ones who give it life. Clinicians who view AI as a partner rather than a threat and AI technologies that enhance rather than replace human competence will rule the future.

A new paradigm in medicine has emerged as a result of this collaboration:

Superintelligent Care = Human Wisdom + Machine Intelligence.

Doctors won't be replaced by AI. It is changing the practice of medicine.

Physicians will:

- Interpret and verify AI findings.
- Explain intricate AI-driven insights to patients.
- When algorithms don't work, use human judgment.
- Make moral choices that a machine cannot.

AI will:

- Examine large amounts of data.
- Identify patterns that are invisible to humans.
- Automate repetitive processes.
- Provide unceasing clinical support.

The "doctor of the future" is someone who understands how to code in a relational rather than a literal sense.

They need to be able to interact with, confront, and question AI.

1.7. A Look toward the Future: The Hospital Enhanced by AI

Imagine a hospital where intelligence permeates every hallway, screen, gadget, and clinical decision. Not in a science-fiction sense, but in a seamless, useful, and life-saving manner.

This is the AI-augmented hospital—a concept that top international institutions are already starting to realize.

This is not a place where doctors are replaced by robots.

It is a place where computers and humans collaborate flawlessly to provide care that is quicker, safer, more accurate, and more compassionate than anything that medicine has ever seen.

1.7.1. An AI-Powered Hospital Day

a. The Command Centre for AI

A real-time "digital nerve centre"—an AI-powered dashboard that tracks:

- Patient flows,
- Vital signs,
- Bed occupancy,
- Emergency surge forecasts,
- Personnel levels,
- Equipment utilization,
- Infection concerns, and
- Even oxygen and drug supplies—is located at the centre of the hospital.

Every potential factor in the hospital's ecology is constantly examined.

The technology immediately identifies a patient on the fifth floor if they start to deteriorate.

The algorithm notifies infection control before any person recognizes a trend if a group of related symptoms points to an impending outbreak.

a. Intelligent Emergency Medical Care

When a patient walks into the emergency department:

1. AI triage rapidly examines facial clues, speech patterns, vitals, and symptoms.
2. The accuracy with which risk scoring systems rank urgency is unparalleled.
3. High-risk patients are sent straight to specialists via fast-lane routing.
4. By automatically creating notes, digital scribes allow physicians to concentrate on their patients.

What used to take forty-five minutes now takes less than five.

1.7.2. Intelligent Diagnostics: Medical Care at Machine Speed

In the AI-enhanced hospital, sophisticated imaging algorithms read scans in a matter of seconds:

- AI may identify illnesses including cancers that are unseen to the human eye, micro strokes, hidden fractures, and early organ decline before human radiologists can.
- AI algorithms trained on millions of samples digitize and co-analyse pathology slides.

- Autonomous analysers that minimize human error and identify irregularities power labs.

Instead of performing clerical tasks, the doctor's function now consists of interpretation, supervision, and individualized decision-making.

1.7.3. Accurate Treatment Schedules Real-time design

Genomics, medical history, lifestyle, biomarkers, imaging data, environmental factors, and pharmaceutical models are all integrated by AI. After that, it creates a customized treatment plan for every patient.

Physicians make adjustments depending on patient preferences, ethics, and their own opinion.

Precision medicine becomes the norm as a result of this synergy and is no longer only speculative.

1.7.4. Automated Healthcare and Robotics

Robotic surgical assistants with tremor-free precision are part of the hospital of the future:

- Real-time drip adjustment using automated infusion pumps.
- Mobile robots that bring lab samples, food, medicine, and linens.
- Smart beds that automatically realign patients based on pressure point detection.
- Virtual nurses that monitor patient comfort and respond to standard inquiries.

Crucially, though, people continue to be at the core; repetitious, dangerous, or physically taxing duties are handled by robots.

1.7.5. Constant Observation Outside the Bedside

In the AI-enhanced hospital, no patient is ever "unseen."

- Heart Rate,
- Respiration Rate,
- Temperature,
- Oxygen Levels,
- Posture, and mobility ..... Are all monitored via wearables, sensors, and ceiling-mounted cameras.

By analysing this data second by second, AI is able to predict:

- Falls Before They Occur;
- Unexpected Cardiac Arrests;
- Septic Shock Hours Beforehand; And
- Respiratory collapse.

Instant alerts enable nurses to take action before a crisis arises.

1.7.6. A Future Focused on Humans

The return of humanity is perhaps the most unexpected aspect of the AI-augmented hospital, not the technology.

AI takes care of:

- Data entry,

- Scheduling,
- Monitoring, and documentation,
- Giving doctors more time to chat with patients,
- Clearly explain diagnoses,
- Establish rapport,
- Reassure families, and
- Make deliberate judgments.

Ironically, AI improves humanity in healthcare—but only if it is applied with compassion and purpose.

1.7.7. The Operational and Ethical Requirements

The foundation of the future AI-enhanced hospital must be:

- **Transparency:** AI choices must be auditable and explicable.
- **Equity:** Diverse populations must be used to train models.
- **Cybersecurity:** Lives depend on the security of every connected device.
- **Accountability**: In the end, clinical results are still the responsibility of humans.
- **Empathy:** A caregiver's therapeutic presence should never be replaced by a machine.

1.7.8. Today Is the First Day of the Hospital of Tomorrow

Leading centres in the United States, Europe, China, and Singapore already have several of these capabilities. In the next five to ten years, more will come. Although it will happen gradually, the shift is unavoidable.

The AI-augmented hospital is the next development in medical technology, not a work of science fiction. AI thinks in a hospital. Physicians take the lead. Patients do well.

This is how healthcare will develop in the future, and your book is preparing the world for it.

In 2035, picture a hospital:

- *Before patients see a nurse, AI triage kiosks evaluate their symptoms.*
- *Vital indicators are continuously streamed to cloud-based AI monitoring by wearable sensors.*
- *Under human supervision, robotic surgical helpers execute precise movements.*
- *Digital twins mimic a patient's reaction to various therapies.*
- *In real time, AI pharmacists verify drug interactions.*
- *Virtual health bots manage chronic illness coaching and follow-ups.*

Nevertheless, the physician continues to be at the centre, directing treatment with empathy and human intuition.

1.8. Conclusion: The AI doctor is here, yet human doctors are more important than ever.

The era of artificial intelligence doctors is arrived. These days, machines are able to scan medical images more quickly than an experienced radiologist, identify tiny genetic changes, process clinical histories at a speed that no human mind can equal, and forecast heart attacks before symptoms manifest.

In many respects, 21st-century algorithms have already surpassed 20th-century doctors. The change cannot be undone. AI is incredibly intelligent, but it lacks a crucial quality that has characterized medicine for thousands of years: *the human doctor's capacity to provide care, reassure, understand context, demonstrate empathy, and eventually take accountability.*

AI is not a cure-all, but it is a very strong tool.

The future is not *"AI Replacing Doctors,"* but rather *"Doctors Using AI Replacing Those Who Don't."*

It's becoming evident that practitioners that use machine intelligence into their workflow will be the most effective.

They will serve more patients more quickly, diagnose more accurately, and treat more precisely. However, the doctor continues to be the ethical, moral, and emotional cornerstone of healthcare. The doctor must determine the meaning of the answer, even if AI provides it.

1.8.1. AI Improves Medicine but Doesn't Humanize It

A mother's anxiety while she awaits her child's test results is beyond the comprehension of a machine.

During a standard consultation, it is unable to detect nonverbal indicators of depression.

An elderly patient who is lonely and just needs a little human interaction cannot be comforted by it.

It is unable to understand trauma, culture, history, or individual preferences.

These human aspects are the foundation of healing; they are not "soft skills."

The clinical process can be guided by technology, but patients can only be guided by humans.

1.8.2. The Role of the Doctor Changes, yet It Only Gets More Crucial.

The duties of a doctor increase rather than decrease as AI becomes more commonplace:

- *To evaluate AI results wisely rather than blindly.*
- *To question algorithms when a deeper truth is suggested by intuition.*
- *To safeguard patient privacy and dignity in an increasingly digital society;*
- *To guarantee justice, openness, and safety.*
- *To continue being the primary source of empathy and the ultimate decision-maker.*

The doctor is now the translator, steward, and protector of machine-derived intelligence rather than the only source of medical knowledge in this new era.

1.8.3. A Collaboration, Not a Substitute

The hospital of the future won't be a chilly place where doctors are replaced by robots.

It is a dynamic collaboration in which technology provide speed, accuracy, and predictive capacity while humans provide judgment, compassion, and moral leadership. *When they work together, they will create a new medical standard that is safer, more intelligent, and more compassionate than anything that has ever been seen.*

1.8.4. The Last Word

AI is revolutionizing healthcare, but it cannot and shouldn't take the role of a human physician. Rather, it makes the physician more capable.

Future doctors won't be afraid of AI; instead, they will be able to control it. The future of medicine may be shaped by AI doctors, but it will be defined by human physicians.

1.8.5. Doctors won't be replaced by AI.

However, physicians that employ AI will take the place of those who don't. In the end, the development of the AI doctor is a tale of collaboration—between algorithmic strength and moral discernment, machine accuracy and human sensitivity.

This book examines that intersection, demonstrating how, with proper risk management, *AI may revolutionize diagnostics, improve patient care, speed up drug discovery, and completely change the healthcare industry.*

Neither humans nor machines will rule the medical field in the future.

Man and machine are involved.

And the future has already started.

Chapter 2: Medical AI's Foundations: How Computers Learn to Heal

Overview

Patients and even some medical professionals may find artificial intelligence to be magical, but every AI system in a hospital, including robotic assistants, diagnostic models, and prediction algorithms, is supported by a structured set of mathematical underpinnings, data pipelines, and human judgment. Healthcare executives, physicians, legislators, and patients must comprehend how AI learns, what it sees, how it thinks, and where it falters.

From machine learning principles to data collection, model training, assessment, and implementation in actual clinical settings, this chapter provides a guided tour of the key components of medical AI. We explore the "mind" of the AI physician, showing how it analyses X-rays, forecasts illness risks, and customizes treatment.

2.1. What Constitutes "Intelligent" AI in Healthcare?

The term "smart" is frequently used to characterize artificial intelligence, but *what precisely makes AI seem clever, particularly in the extremely complicated and dangerous field of medicine?* The fact is both straightforward and profound: AI becomes intelligent not because it "thinks" like a human doctor, but rather because it is superior to human minds in terms of patterns, forecasts, and accuracy.

2.1.1. Superhuman-Scale Pattern Recognition

Medical data is enormous, disorganized, and dense—much more than a clinician can manually process. AI systems gain intelligence by discovering patterns in millions of medical photos, thousands of patient records, genomic sequences, clinical notes and lab findings, and real-time vital signs. An AI reading a chest X-ray, for instance, compares the image to millions of images it has already seen. This enables it to identify minute textures, shadows, or irregularities that even skilled radiologists could overlook.

2.1.2. Continuous Learning from Data

AI becomes better with each new piece of information. *An AI model can be trained on 20 years' worth of emergency room data, tens of thousands of cancer cases, and billions of biological interactions, but a human doctor depends on decades' worth of experience.* This enormous "experience bank" enables AI to provide recommendations based on a constantly updated, nearly encyclopaedic memory.

2.1.3. Predictive Intelligence

AI does more than merely examine past events. It predicts what is likely to occur.

Examples include:

- Identifying future mental health crises based on modest behavioural changes;
- Predicting who is at danger of cardiac arrest hours before symptoms occur;
- Forecasting sepsis before vital signs worsen; and
- Estimating therapy responses based on molecular signatures.

AI is now proactive rather than merely diagnostic thanks to this predictive understanding, which changes medicine from reactive to preventive.

2.1.4. Combining Different Knowledge Sources

A human physician is able to balance several things at once. AI is capable of juggling thousands at once. Imaging data, electronic health records (EHR), wearable device data, genomic and proteomic data, drug interaction databases, and clinical recommendations are all integrated by modern AI. In complicated decision-making, AI appears nearly superhuman due to its capacity to "think in thousands."

2.1.5. Objective Reasoning in Mathematics

Fatigue, emotion, stress, and cognitive biases all affect human cognition. When AI is properly designed, it only uses mathematics to evaluate data. It doesn't:

- Assume things,
- Grow weary,

- Omit steps, or
- Forget specifics.

Because of its dependability, it works very well in situations like emergency response, triage, and high-pressure decision-making.

2.1.6. The Delusion of Intelligence Accuracy + Speed

The "intelligence" of AI frequently seems magical because it combines:

- Large memory capacity,
- Microsecond processing speed,
- Mathematically optimized decision-making, and
- Almost instantaneous pattern matching

The true secret, however, is that AI is intelligent in a computer sense rather than a human one.

Additionally, such type of intelligence can occasionally outperform human intuition in the field of medicine.

2.1.7. Intelligence via Collaboration

AI excels when it enhances medical professionals rather than when it replaces them.

It provides:

- A second set of eyes;
- A safety net against overlooking;
- A prediction engine;
- A reliable, impartial assessor; and

- An unceasing helper 24/7.

Because of this synergy, a new hybrid form of expertise—Doctor + AI—is created that produces better results than each could on its own.

Diagram: How AI becomes Intelligent in Medicine

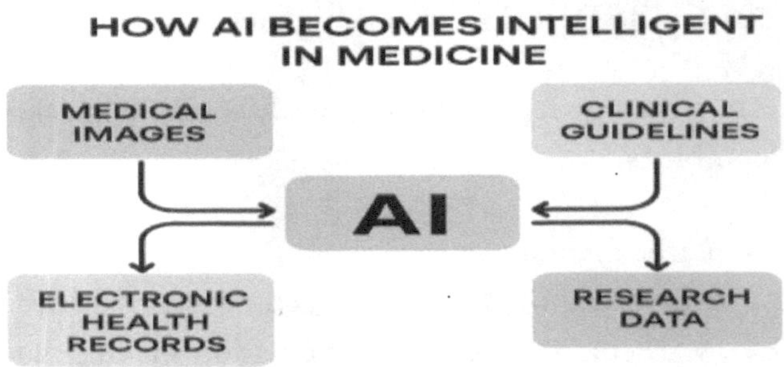

Figure 1: How AI becomes Intelligent in Medicine

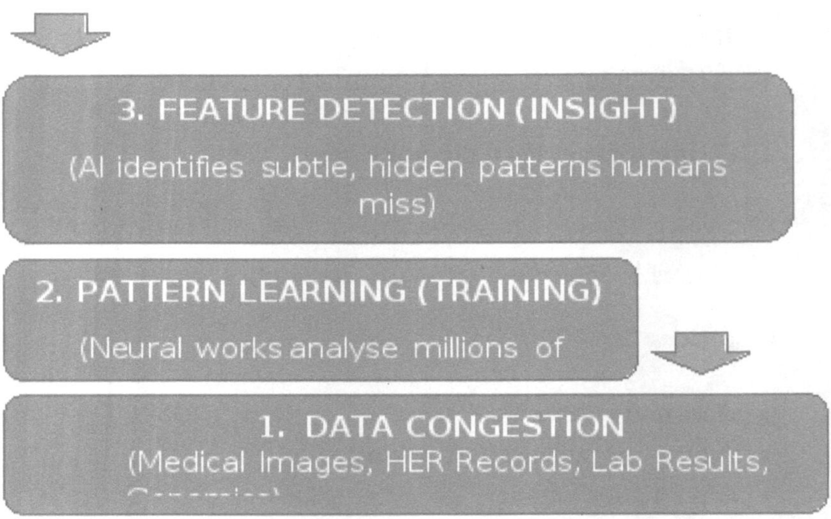

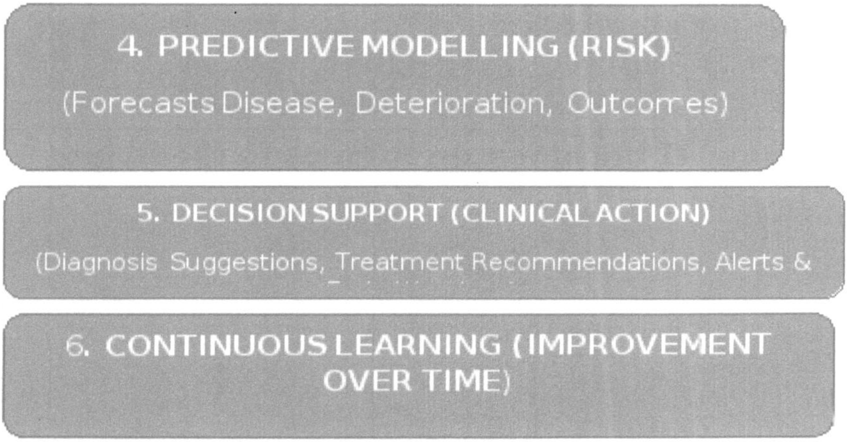
4. PREDICTIVE MODELLING (RISK)
(Forecasts Disease, Deterioration, Outcomes)
5. DECISION SUPPORT (CLINICAL ACTION)
(Diagnosis Suggestions, Treatment Recommendations, Alerts &
6. CONTINUOUS LEARNING (IMPROVEMENT OVER TIME)

Figure 2: How AI becomes Intelligent in Medicine (Amplified)

2.2. The Source of Knowledge for Medical AI

Although AI may seem intelligent, its strength stems from the breadth, depth, and calibre of the data it is taught on. Medical AI learns from enormous datasets that greatly outweigh a single lifetime of human exposure, in contrast to a human doctor who learns from textbooks, mentors, and clinical practice. These data sources make up the "knowledge base" that enables AI systems to make increasingly accurate diagnoses, predictions, and recommendations.

2.2.1. Medical Images

Imaging data is one of the most abundant sources of AI expertise.

X-rays, MRIs, CT scans, ultrasound pictures, and digital pathology slides are used to train AI models. AI gains the ability to identify minute irregularities—patterns that even skilled radiologists might overlook—using millions of annotated instances. This is the basis for "superhuman" medical imaging pattern recognition.

2.2.2. Electronic Health Records (EHR)

A lifetime of patient data is stored in EHRs, including:

- Lab findings;
- Prescriptions;
- Symptoms and clinical notes;
- Diagnoses; and
- Treatment results.

AI can identify connections that people miss when trained on this data at scale, such as odd symptom clusters, uncommon medicine interactions, or long-term deterioration trends.

2.2.3. Diagnostic and Laboratory Data

Because it is accurate and reliable, structured lab data is a treasure trove for artificial intelligence. Blood tests, biomarker levels, metabolic panels, hormonal assays, and microbiological results are a few examples. These allow AI to forecast illness onset, progression, and response to treatment in great detail.

2.2.4. Molecular and Genomic Data

AI is learning more and more from whole-genome sequencing, proteomics, metabolomics, and gene expression patterns as precision medicine expands. Personalized treatment plans are made possible by AI's ability to recognize the molecular signatures of diseases, particularly cancer, thanks to these datasets.

2.2.5. Real-Time Monitoring And Wearables

Smart watches, continuous glucose monitoring, heart-rate sensors, blood-oxygen monitors, and sleep trackers are just a few examples of the data that modern medical AI continuously learns from. AI can identify early warning indicators of cardiac events, respiratory distress, and glucose instability thanks to this real-time feed.

2.2.6. Clinical Guidelines and Medical Literature

Clinical trial findings, pharmaceutical studies, peer-reviewed medical journals, and treatment guidelines (WHO, CDC, FDA, NICE) are among the sources of information used by advanced models, particularly in natural language processing (NLP).

Because of this, AI can stay current with medical information far more quickly than human practitioners.

2.2.7. Physician Input and Expert Annotations

AI doesn't learn on its own. It is taught by human specialists. Physicians make contributions by labelling pictures, flagging accurate or inaccurate predictions, establishing clinical thresholds, and offering input on actual cases.

This "human-in-the-loop" strategy guarantees that AI knowledge represents clinical realities rather than merely mathematical patterns.

2.2.8. Practical Clinical Outcomes

AI systems continue to learn from patient outcomes, treatment efficacy, physician adjustments, and system feedback loops when they are implemented in hospitals. This makes the AI more intelligent over time by converting each clinical interaction into fresh knowledge.

2.2.9. Crucial Perspective

The medical intelligence of AI is not magical; rather, it is the result of enormous, varied, and constantly changing datasets.

The AI's power increases with the accuracy of the data.

Figure: Where AI in Medicine Gets Its Knowledge

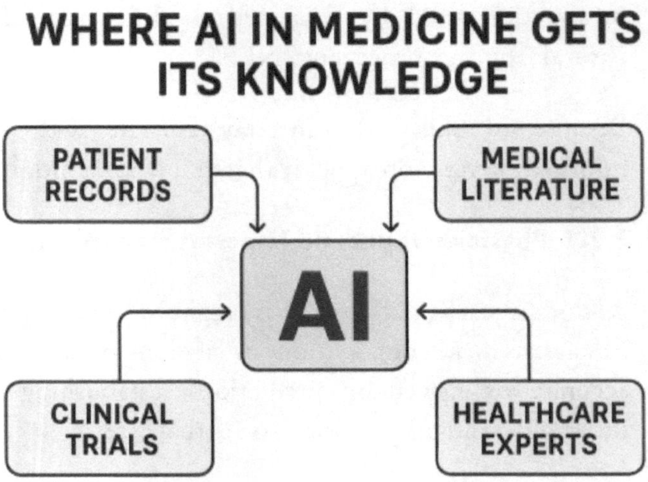

Figure 3: Where AI in Medicine Gets Its Knowledge

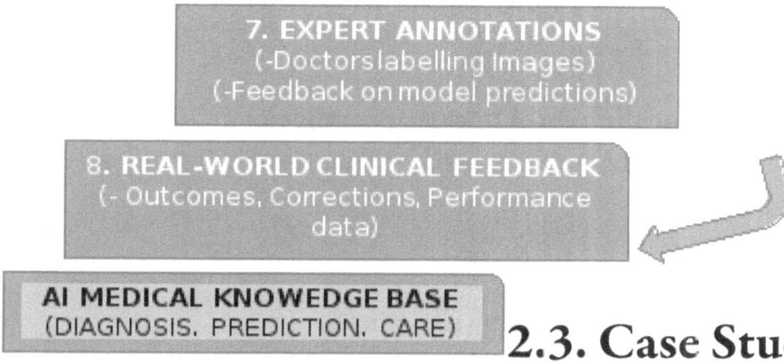

2.3. Case Study: How an AI Model Acquires the Ability to Identify Lung Cancer

Imagine a real-world situation where an AI system is trained to identify lung cancer using CT images in order to comprehend how medical AI becomes truly "intelligent." Despite being one of the deadliest diseases in the world, lung cancer survival rates soar when detected early. The problem is that even skilled radiologists might readily overlook early-stage cancers since they are small and faint.

Because of this, lung cancer diagnosis is the ideal illustration of how AI learns, develops, and finally surpasses human pattern recognition.

Step 1: Gathering the Unprocessed Data

Hundreds of thousands of chest CT images are provided by a group of hospitals, and thoracic radiologists classify each scan.

Every scan consists of:

- Tumours (with precise limits defined by specialists);
- Benign nodules;
- Healthy lungs;
- Differences in age, Ethnicity, Architecture, and underlying problems.

AI can only learn from what it sees, therefore the dataset needs to be big and varied.

Step 2: Educating the AI the Appearance of a Tumour
The photographs are annotated by radiologists, who mark:

- The size,
- Form, and
- Texture patterns of the tumour.
- The behaviour of surrounding tissues, and
- The direction of growth.

By providing the AI with clear instances of "this is cancer" and "this is not cancer," these annotations serve as the teacher.

Subtle traits are first identified by the AI model, which is typically a convolutional neural network (CNN):

- Soft tissue with ripple-like patterns;
- Irregular edges;
- Slight variations in density;
- Patterns of microvascular.

The human eye cannot reliably identify these features because they are too faint or too small.

Step 3: Iteration Teaches the Model
The AI repeatedly contrasts its predictions with the radiologist-labelled truth as it is being trained.
Cycle following cycle:

1. The AI determines if a certain area is malignant.
2. Accuracy is verified by the system using expert labelling.

3. Errors are computed.
4. The AI modifies its own settings.
5. The cycle is repeated thousands of times.

AI learning is powered by a mechanism known as back propagation.

The model improves in accuracy, confidence, and sensitivity to minute patterns over time.

Step 4: New Patient Validation

The AI is tested on never-before-seen CT scans to guarantee real-world dependability.

The following are important evaluation metrics:

- **Sensitivity:** The ability to identify actual tumours.
- **Specificity:** The degree to which it prevents false alarms.
- **False-positive rate:** Important to prevent needless biopsies.
- **Consistency:** The same outcome each and every time.

The model is retrained if it does poorly in any category.

Step 5: Implementation in a Medical Environment

The AI becomes a diagnostic assistant when used in a healthcare setting.

This is how it actually operates:

1. A standard CT scan is performed on a patient.
2. The scan is analysed by the AI in a matter of seconds.
3. It draws attention to suspicious areas and frequently detects nodules as small as 3–5 mm.
4. It uses learnt features to assign a risk score to each nodule.
5. Using AI as a second reader, the radiologist makes the ultimate decision.

This hybrid technique improves accuracy, particularly in early detection, but it does not take the role of a doctor.

Step 6: Ongoing Education

Physicians routinely:

- Accept or reject AI recommendations;
- Provide updated annotations when more scans are examined in actual hospitals.
- Update the system with updated patient outcomes.

Over time, this real-world feedback loops back into training, strengthening and improving the AI's accuracy.

Case Example: The Life Saved

A CT scan is performed on a middle-aged guy who has been coughing nonstop. Nothing concerning is seen by the radiologist. However, the AI draws attention to a tiny lump that is only 4 mm and hardly noticeable.

Risk score: *High likelihood of adenocarcinoma in its early stages.*

The AI's suspicion is validated by a biopsy.

When the tumour is still tiny and localized, it is excised.

Without AI, the cancer might not have been discovered for another year, which could have been too late for a viable course of therapy.

An Overview of the Insight

AI learns to identify lung cancer by analysing thousands of expert-labelled instances, honing its predictions, and gaining insight from actual results rather than by magic.

This is the pinnacle of machine intelligence: superhuman-scale, life-saving accuracy.

2.4. Case Study: Diabetic Retinopathy Identification in Remote Villages

One of the main causes of blindness in the globe is diabetic retinopathy (DR). However, the late diagnosis—rather than the illness itself—is the tragedy. Many rural towns lack retinal imaging specialists, ophthalmologists, and dependable transportation to urban hospitals. Until it is too late to preserve their vision, patients suffer from gradual vision loss.

This is when AI starts to change people's lives.

The Problem: No Medical Professionals, No Diagnostics

Diabetes is on the rise in isolated villages in Asia and Africa, yet there is almost no retinal screening.

The closest eye clinic may be 200 kilometres away from a patient's home. The illness has progressed by the time symptoms like dark spots and blurred vision show up.

A qualified ophthalmologist, specialized retinal imaging equipment, and follow-up visits are all necessary for traditional screening.

Rural health posts do not have these conditions.

Step 1: Introducing AI Screening to the Community

AI-powered retinal diagnosis tool is implemented by a global health NGO in collaboration with regional clinics.

A portable smartphone-based fundus camera, a solar charger, and an AI model connected to the cloud that has been trained on millions of retinal photos are given to each clinic.

During routine examinations, a nurse or community health worker with no experience in ophthalmology captures retinal images of diabetic patients.

The AI evaluates the pictures in a matter of seconds.

Step 2: The AI's Disease Recognition

Millions of annotated retinal photos from hospitals all over the world are used to train the AI model.

It gains the ability to recognize:

- Micro aneurysms;
- Bleeding;
- Cotton wool spots, and
- hard exudates
- Retinal enema and ischemic regions;
- Neovascularization (new, brittle blood vessels).

In the early stages, these patterns are frequently imperceptible to non-specialists.

Each eye is given a classification by the AI:

- No DR;
- Mild;
- Moderate;
- Severe;
- Proliferative DR (urgent)

Additionally, it produces a recommendation for referrals.

Step 3: Actual People, Actual Effects

Joseph, a 52-year-old farmer, travels to a remote village for a diabetes examination.

He has never had a retinal damage screening, like many others.

The nurse uses the portable camera to take pictures of his retina.

In five seconds, the AI detects:

"Immediate Referral Needed for Severe Non-Proliferative Diabetic Retinopathy."

Joseph has not yet experienced any vision loss or eye pain.

He would have probably become blind in a year or two if there had been no screening.

Due to the AI's early detection of the illness:

- A regional hospital is recommended for him;
- Blindness is avoided;
- Laser treatment is administered;

Just one picture.
Just one diagnosis.
One person's life was transformed.

Step 4: Changing Health Systems in Rural Areas

AI changes entire health ecosystems, not just specific patients.

Prior to AI:

- High blindness rates;
- Long travel distances;
- Less than 5% of diabetic people were evaluated;
- Delays in diagnosis

Following AI:

- More than 80% of patients are screened each year;
- Local clinics provide instant triage;
- Only high-risk patients are referred to distant hospitals;
- There is a significant decrease in avoidable blindness

AI, according to medical professionals, lessens referral overload, freeing up doctors to concentrate on patients who actually require immediate care.

Step 5: Ongoing Education Increases Precision

- Every new retinal scan, every confirmed diagnosis, and
- Every treatment result goes back into the AI model as more communities use the system.

Future patients, particularly those in the most remote communities, will find the system more accurate thanks to this "global learning loop."

Crucial Perspective

In underprivileged areas, AI does not take the position of doctors; rather, it serves as their eyes while they are far away.

AI-powered diabetic retinopathy screening transforms blindness from an inevitable condition into a preventive one for isolated tribes.

2.5. Natural Language Processing: Interpreting Medical Notes

Every hospital has a pile of unstructured text—clinicians' free-form notes—behind every diagnosis and lab result. The deepest insights about a patient's story can be found in these notes, including the patient's own description of their symptoms, the doctor's clinical reasoning, subtle risk factors, and historical information that is rarely found in structured databases. However, machines were mostly unable to reach this golden mine for decades.

That has been altered by Natural Language Processing (NLP). The branch of artificial intelligence known as *Natural Language Processing (NLP)* enables computers to comprehend, interpret, and derive meaning from human language. It transforms disorganized, handwritten, shorthand-heavy narratives into organized, practical intelligence in the medical field.

1. **Why It's So Difficult for Machines to Understand Clinical Note**

Machine parsing of clinical notes is infamously challenging since they are:

- **Unstructured:** free text that frequently lacks formatting.
- **Packed with medical jargon**, such as "SOB," "r/o PE," and "HTN x 5y."
- **Rich in acronyms and abbreviations**, many of which overlap; highly contextual (for example, "patient denies chest pain" indicates the lack of a symptom);
- **Written in different formats** by different departments and professionals.

To provide trustworthy insight, NLP models must overcome all of these obstacles.

1. **NLP's Use of Clinical Notes**

Several potent tasks can be completed by contemporary NLP systems:

1. **Extraction of Entities**

Finding important clinical components like:

- Symptoms;
- Drugs;
- Diagnosis;
- Allergies;
- Lab values;
- Procedures.

For instance, NLP can extract the following from the line "Pt presents with severe dyspnoea; rule out CHF":

Dyspnoea is a *symptom.*

Congestive heart failure is the *suspected diagnosis.*

1. **Interpretation of Context (Very Important in Medicine)**

LP makes a distinction between:

- Negated conditions ("denies chest pain");
- Present conditions ("has chest pain");
- Family history ("mother had breast cancer");
- Historical circumstances ("history of TB");

- Prearranged activities ("CT scan scheduled").

Clinical NLP differs from standard text processing because of this contextual intelligence.

1. **Synopsis and Remark**

On-the-spot patient summaries, structured EMR fields, discharge notes, and referral letters can all be produced by AI.

Clinicians save hours every day, which lessens documentation fatigue and burnout.

1. **Risk Forecasting and Pattern Identification**

NLP algorithms can identify patterns that people often overlook by examining thousands or even millions of notes. These patterns include:

- Early indicators of sepsis from modest wording;
- Mental health risk indicators (e.g., linguistic patterns predicting suicidal ideation); and
- Correlations between symptoms and future consequences.

Certain systems are better at predicting hospital readmission risk based on notes than on lab results alone.

Example: NLP's Use in an Emergency Room

Note from the patient: "The patient, a 58-year-old man who smokes heavily, has a worsening cough, night sweats, and weight loss. Denies experiencing chest pain. Lung cancer claimed the father's life.

NLP results:

- Symptoms include weight loss, coughing, and nocturnal sweats.
- Risk factors include a family history of lung cancer and heavy smoking.
- Chest pain is absent.
- Possible warning signs include a high suspicion of cancer or tuberculosis.
- Triage recommendation: immediate imaging is advised.

This immediately transforms a single paragraph of text into organized, useful data.

The Reasons NLP Is Changing Healthcare

NLP unlocks the single largest store of clinical information because 70–80% of all medical data is locked in text. Faster diagnosis, more precise risk assessment, less effort for clinicians, more patient safety, and increased public health insights are the outcomes.

Clinical documentation is becoming a living intelligence system with real-time learning, prediction, and care assistance thanks to NLP.

2.6. Large Language Models (LLMs) in Healthcare

LLMs are the greatest revolutionary advancement in medical AI to date. While previous AI systems were excellent at specific tasks, such as identifying a tumour on a scan, identifying abnormal test results, or categorizing retinal images, LLMs provide something completely different: large-scale general medical reasoning. *Trillions of words from medical textbooks, clinical recommendations, research publications, and de-identified clinical notes are used to train these models.* They *thus acquire* nearly professional proficiency in their comprehension, interpretation, and production of human language.

This implies that LLMs are capable of reading, writing, summarizing, translating, reasoning, and even suggesting future steps in therapeutic settings—a capability that was previously unthinkable.

LLMs are neither physicians nor their substitutes. However, they are becoming into strong cognitive allies that can enhance human medical intelligence.

1. **What Distinguishes LLMs from Conventional Medical AI**

1. **They Recognize Context**

LLMs are capable of interpreting complicated, unstructured, and nuanced patient data, such as "intermittent crushing chest pain radiating to the left arm," "feels dizzy when standing," and "not responding well to current medication," in contrast to rule-based or task-specific models.

They are able to make connections between risk factors, history, and symptoms.

1. They Are Capable of Doing Several Things at Once

LLMs can concurrently:

- Summarize patient histories;
- Draft clinical notes;
- Interpret lab results;
- Respond to medical inquiries;
- Convert speech to structured data;
- Extract symptoms and diagnoses;
- Translate between languages; and
- Assist in clinical decision-making, whereas previous AI systems were only capable of one task.

Hospitals are integrating them across workflows due to their multi-capability.

1. They Use Human Language to Reason

LLMs can explain how an illness develops, why a diagnosis is likely, and why a therapy could be recommended.

People trust them more than "black box" AI algorithms because of their interpretability.

1. Fundamental Uses of LLMs in Healthcare

1. Clinical Documentation Automation

LLMs help physicians by creating complete clinical notes, summarizing interactions, creating discharge summaries, and turning discussions into organized EMR fields.

Documentation time can be cut by 50–70% only by doing this.

1. **Assistance with Clinical Decisions**

LLMs may recommend:

- Differential diagnoses, tests to order, red flags that need to be checked out, and treatment options based on guidelines.
- They provide as knowledgeable second opinions, but human confirmation is always necessary.

1. **Communication with Patients**

LLMs offer:

- Help from chatbots;
- Post-surgery instructions;
- Symptom triage;
- Medication explanations;
- Education about chronic illnesses.

They increase access to healthcare, particularly in places where there is a shortage of clinicians.

1. **Acceleration of Medical Research**

Researchers can use LLMs to summarize thousands of publications, create hypotheses, categorize studies, transform PDFs into structured databases, and expedite drug discovery processes.

In a few of minutes, certain LLMs are capable of analysing entire scientific domains.

1. Intelligence from EMR

By reading complete medical records, recognizing neglected symptoms, extracting important risks, and forecasting outcomes from narrative notes, LLMs help close the gap between organized and unstructured data.

They transform the EMR into a system of living knowledge.

An example of an LLM-assisted diagnosis in an emergency room.

The following is noted by a triage nurse:

"72-year-old female with confusion, mild fever, decreased urine output; on diuretics; history of CKD."

Upon reviewing the note, an LLM may identify:

- Potential Urosepsis;
- Acute kidney injury risk;
- Possible medication-induced dehydration;
- Recommendations: urgent vitals, CBC, renal panel, and cultures.

The model speeds up clinical awareness but does not diagnose.

1. LLMs' Drawbacks and Dangers in Medicine

LLMs are powerful, but they must be used carefully:

1. **Delusions**: Sometimes LLMs make confident but inaccurate claims. If left uncontrolled, this might be hazardous.

2. **Prejudice**: Bias in the training data could be reflected in the model:

- Underdiagnosing specific groups.
- Excessively flagging others.

3. **Privacy Concerns**: Safely handling medical data is essential, particularly when fine-tuning.

4. **Ethical and Legal Limitations**: *If an LLM's recommendation causes harm, who is at fault?*

The world is still debating this issue.

1. AI-Doctor Collaboration: An Emerging Trend

LLMs exist to increase human capabilities, not to take the position of doctors. An AI helper will be incorporated into each process in the hospital of the future:

Listening during sessions; automatically updating records; exposing hidden hazards; making recommendations based on evidence; and keeping an eye on patient data in real time

An LLM makes a doctor more precise, knowledgeable, and productive.

2.7. Comprehending Failure Modes, Bias, and Model Accuracy

In the medical field, artificial intelligence can be incredibly potent, yet it is not perfect. Clinicians, administrators, and legislators must comprehend how models work, where they fall short, and how bias might infiltrate in order to employ AI safely and efficiently. These considerations directly affect patient outcomes, trust, and the legal and ethical deployment of AI in healthcare.

1. **Model Accuracy: Performance Evaluation**

The accuracy of an AI model varies depending on the job and metric:

- **Sensitivity (True Positive Rate):** Indicates how well the model finds real disease cases. In life-threatening illnesses like cancer or sepsis, high sensitivity minimizes missed diagnoses.
- **Specificity (True Negative Rate)**: Evaluates the model's ability to recognize healthy patients. High specificity lowers false alarms, which can save money, stress, and needless treatments.
- **Accuracy (Positive Predictive Value)**: *How many of the anticipated positive instances are actually positive?*
    - Low precision models lead to needless follow-ups.
    - Recall quantifies the proportion of actual cases to the number of true cases the model detects. A high recall guarantees that important circumstances are not missed.
- **Total Precision**: Percentage of all cases with accurate forecasts. A helpful statistic, but in unbalanced datasets (such as uncommon disorders), it may be deceptive on its own.

1. Bias: When AI Acquires Inaccurate Knowledge

When an AI model consistently favours or discriminates against particular groups, this is known as bias. Bias in medicine can result from:

- **Unbalanced Training Data:** For instance, an AI that was mostly trained on photos of patients with lighter skin tones may perform poorly on patients with darker skin tones, failing to detect dermatological disorders or melanoma.
- **Historical Clinical Bias:** The AI may underdiagnose underprivileged populations if prior clinical decisions exhibited socioeconomic bias.
- **Bias in Feature Selection:** The model may rely too much on unrelated patterns if some input variables are overrepresented or underrepresented.

The effects of bias:

- Inaccurate or overlooked diagnosis;
- Inequitable treatment for different populations;
- Ethical and legal ramifications.

It takes diligent auditing, ongoing monitoring, and a variety of sample datasets to mitigate bias.

1. Failure Modes: How and Why AI Might Fail

Unexpected failures can happen to even the most successful AI. Typical failure modes consist of:

a. **Out-of-Distribution (OOD) Data:** AI performs poorly when it comes across data that is substantially different from its training set. For instance, a chest X-ray AI that was trained on adult patients might not work on photos of children.

b. **Adversarial Inputs**: AI can become confused by tiny, frequently undetectable changes in input data:

- Misclassification may result from slightly changed radiographs or noise in digital pictures.

a. **Excessive fitting:** Because it memorized rather than generalized patterns, a model may perform flawlessly on training data but poorly on new patients.
b. **Noise from Labels:** AI predictions are impacted by mistakes in the training dataset, such as incorrectly tagged photos or notes.
c. **Misinterpretation of Context:** AI may mistake vague language or uncommon clinical circumstances. For instance, if the model is unable to identify negation, "No evidence of infection" may be misinterpreted as positive.

1. **Tracking AI Performance in Real-World Applications**

Continuous monitoring is necessary for the safe deployment of AI:

- **Audits of Performance:** Check the sensitivity, specificity, and error rates of various patient groups on a regular basis.
- **Bias Assessments:** Monitor results for comorbidities, age, gender, and race.
- **Feedback loops:** Retrain and enhance models by including patient outcomes and clinician modifications.
- **Stress Evaluation**: Test AI in edge cases, uncommon circumstances, and unusual presentations.

1. **Crucial Realization: Understanding Builds Trust**

AI is not a secret, magical machine. Data, algorithms, and human control are the sources of its "intelligence."

For safe deployment, it is crucial to comprehend accuracy, bias, and failure mechanisms.

AI must be viewed by clinicians as a potent tool rather than an indisputable oracle.

2.8. The Reasons AI Occasionally Produces "Weird" Errors

AI in medicine has the potential to be incredibly accurate, detecting tumours that are too small for the human eye to see, anticipating problems before symptoms manifest, and quickly triaging patients. However, even the most advanced models occasionally produce strange, nonsensical, or wholly unexpected mistakes. For the safe and efficient application of AI in healthcare, *it is essential to comprehend why these "weird" errors occur.*

1. **AI Identifies Patterns Rather Than Causes**

AI does not fully comprehend illness, in contrast to human physicians. It *does not reason about physiology, context, or causality; instead, it finds connections and patterns in data.* For instance, an AI model that was taught to identify pneumonia on chest X-rays once tagged pictures with cables or text artefacts as "pneumonia." Why? Many pneumonia X-rays contained monitor wires or hospital labels in the same location during training. Unaware that these items were unimportant, the AI connected them to illness. The AI picks up on characteristics that are statistically correlated but clinically useless; this is commonly referred to as "shortcut learning."

1. **Not in Distribution Inputs**

AI works best with data that is similar to what it has seen in training. Strange mistakes may occur if the input varies considerably.

Examples include:

- MRI scans from a new machine with slightly changed imaging parameters;
- Paediatric X-rays supplied to a model trained on adults.
- Unusual manifestations of uncommon illnesses.

Predictions that are obviously incorrect to a human expert may be confidently made by the model.

1. **Medical Data Ambiguity and Noise**

Medical data is disorganized. Typos, abbreviations, unclear terminology, and missing information can all be found in patient records. These anomalies could be misinterpreted or overemphasized by AI. For instance, if the AI is unable to identify negation, clinical notes that state "no evidence of infection" may be misinterpreted, leading to a false-positive infection warning.

1. **Overconfidence in the Model**

Overconfidence can cause AI algorithms to attribute a high probability to inaccurate predictions. AI does not typically adjust confidence based on context and uncertainty, unlike humans.

For instance, even though a rare retinal illness is clinically distinct, a diabetic retinopathy AI may confidently categorize it as "severe DR" since the visual patterns appear to be similar to what it has seen during training.

1. **Insufficient Common Sense**

Humans make unlikely or impossible diagnoses using their intuition and general knowledge. This kind of common sense reasoning is absent from AI.

For instance, it is obviously absurd for an AI to predict "male pregnancy" from unclear lab notes, but statistically the data may appear to fit patterns acquired from other settings.

1. **Edge and Adversarial Situations**

AI can occasionally become confused by minute, undetectable changes in input.

In adversarial scenarios, this is typical: Small pixel value shifts; slight noise in an image; and subtle text formatting alterations Even for high-performing models, this can result in radically inaccurate outputs.

1. **Important Takeaway: Strange Errors Are Unavoidable, Not Unacceptable**

AI is strong, yet it lacks intelligence. When statistical reasoning is applied to complicated, flawed, high-dimensional data, errors naturally result.

Human oversight, ongoing monitoring, awareness of the model's limitations, and systems built to detect improbable or "weird" outputs are all necessary for safe AI in medicine.

Knowing why AI makes odd errors is a guide to using the technology sensibly, not a criticism of it. Clinicians can utilize AI's superhuman skills while avoiding potentially hazardous blind spots when they are aware of these peculiarities.

2.9. Data Security, Privacy, and Ethical Issues

Healthcare is changing as a result of artificial intelligence, but there are also significant new obligations. Large volumes of sensitive patient data, including lab findings, wearable device readings, clinical notes, imaging, and genomic data, are essential to medical AI. It is both morally and legally required to protect this data. AI abuse, breaches, or unethical use can worsen inequality, jeopardize patient trust, and possibly put lives in danger.

1. **Data Privacy: Safeguarding Patient Identity**

   The cornerstone of moral healthcare is patient privacy. AI models need to respect privacy:

   - **De-identification:** Eliminating identifiers from datasets, such as names and addresses.
   - **Anonymisation:** Ensuring that even indirect data points cannot be used to re-identify patients.
   - **Consent**: Patients must be made aware of the usage of their data for AI research or training and must give their consent.
   - **Data Minimization**: To reduce exposure, only gather the information required for the AI task.

   Legal repercussions (such as HIPAA in the US and GDPR in the EU) and a decline in public confidence might result from a failure to protect privacy.

1. **Security of Data: Protecting Sensitive Data**

Because of its worth and sensitivity, healthcare data is a major target for cyberattacks. Further security issues are introduced by AI systems:

- **Encryption:** To prevent unwanted access, data must be encrypted both in transit and at rest.
- **Access Controls:** AI systems and patient data should only be accessible by authorized individuals.
- **Audit Trails:** Keeping track of who accessed data, when, and why aids in the detection and prevention of breaches.
- **Safe AI Implementation:** To stop data leaks and manipulation, cloud-based AI needs to employ strong security measures.

The personal and medical data of thousands of people could be compromised by a single hack.

1. AI's Ethical Considerations

Beyond security and privacy, AI in healthcare presents special ethical issues:

a. Fairness and Bias

Health inequities may be sustained by AI algorithms trained on unrepresentative datasets:

- Unequal access to AI-driven healthcare;
- Underdiagnosis in minority communities;
- Overdiagnosis in specific demographics.

Diverse data, fairness audits, and continuous monitoring are necessary for mitigation.

a. **Responsibility and Accountability**

If AI makes a dangerous advice, who is in charge?

- Institutions, clinicians, and developers are all accountable.

When human monitoring is required must be specified in clear policies.

a. **Explainability and Transparency**

AI cannot function as a "black box":

- Patients and clinicians should be aware of how AI arrived at a judgment.
- Explainable AI promotes ethical accountability, lowers errors, and builds trust.

a. **Autonomy and Consent**

In AI-driven healthcare, patients ought to have a choice:

- Choosing whether to receive AI-assisted treatment.
- Being aware of the advantages and disadvantages of AI recommendations.

Improving results is just as important as respecting patient autonomy.

a. **Long-Term Consequences**

- AI has the potential to alter medical decision-making power, workflows, and roles.
- Changes in the patient-doctor relationship and the influence

on the workforce are two factors that ethical deployment must take into account.

- The impact of automated healthcare decisions on society

1. Useful Steps for Implementing Ethical AI

To strike a balance between creativity and accountability:

1. **Create Governance Structures:** Committees to examine data policies, prejudice, and AI ethics.
2. **Conduct Frequent Audits**: Constantly keep an eye on bias, security, and privacy.
3. **Educate Staff**: Make sure medical professionals are aware of the potential and constraints of AI.
4. **Involve Patients:** Clearly explain how AI is used in diagnosis and treatment.
5. **Employ Privacy-Preserving AI:** Methods like differential privacy and federated learning lower risk.

1. Crucial Perspective

AI has the potential to completely transform healthcare, but only if it is combined with strict privacy regulations, strong security, and moral awareness.

For AI in medicine to be safe, efficient, and reliable, patient data protection, equity, and accountability are essential.

2.10. Human + AI: A Joint Approach to Healthcare

In the medical field, artificial intelligence is frequently misinterpreted as a substitute for human physicians. In actuality, human-AI cooperation is the most successful paradigm. Together, they combine the speed, accuracy, and pattern recognition of AI with the advantages of human judgment, empathy, and context. Healthcare delivery is changing as a result of this mixed strategy.

1. The Benefits of Collaboration over Replacement

AI and humans complement each other's strengths:

Humans	**AI**
Profound contextual awareness	Superhuman ability to recognize patterns
Empathy and emotional intelligence	Continuous large-scale data analysis
Moral judgment and ethical reasoning	Quick identification of irregularities in pictures, laboratories, and notes
Intuition and experience	Reliability and lack of weariness
Capacity to manage uncommon, new situations	Finding minor trends via learning from large datasets

Figure 4: The Benefits of Collaboration over Replacement

Note: Hospitals can improve patient outcomes, diagnosis speed, and accuracy by combining these qualities.

1. Collaborative Workflows in Practice

a. Diagnostic Support

- AI identifies abnormalities in lab, imaging, or vital signs.

- Physicians examine AI recommendations and relate them to the patient's medical history.
- The ultimate choice combines human judgment with technological accuracy.

For instance, in a lung CT scan, an AI indicates a small nodule. After examining the area and determining its relevance, the radiologist chooses whether to perform further imaging.

a. **Clinical Documentation:**

- AI uses electronic records or dictation to create structured notes.
- Clinicians check and revise summaries, giving context and subtlety.
  This maintains accuracy and customization while lessening the load of documentation.

a. **Treatment Planning:**

- AI may forecast patient response or recommend medicines based on guidelines.
- Clinicians take into account comorbidities, personal preferences, and ethical issues.

For instance, AI in oncology forecasts how a tumour will react to various chemotherapy treatments. Taking the patient's quality of life and side effects into account, the oncologist selects the optimal course of action.

1. **Improving Patient Interaction**

AI can free up time for medical professionals:

- Automating repetitive processes;
- Summarizing patient records; and
- Sending out notifications and reminders.

This enables medical professionals to concentrate on patient education, empathy, and listening—tasks that AI cannot duplicate.

1. **Constant Education Collectively**

Collaboration is dynamic; people learn from AI ideas, while AI becomes better with feedback:

- AI gains knowledge from clinicians' corrections and results.
- Clinicians learn about risk factors or subtle trends that they were previously unaware of.

As a result, a feedback loop is created in which computer and human intelligence complement one another.

1. **Actual Example: Triage in the Emergency Department**

1. A patient comes in complaining about chest pain.
2. AI flags a high-risk profile for myocardial infarction by analysing vitals, ECG, and previous data.
3. After reviewing the AI's alert, the triage nurse assigns the patient a priority for prompt testing.
4. The emergency physician assesses the patient while taking the patient's context and comorbidities into account.

As a result, human judgment guarantees safe, individualized care while AI speeds up danger identification.

1. **Essential Guidelines for Human-AI Cooperation**

1. **AI as Assistant, Not Authority**: Humans make decisions, while machines offer recommendations.
2. **Transparent AI:** To trust suggestions, clinicians must comprehend AI logic.
3. **Constant Feedback**: AI receives corrections from humans to increase learning.
4. **Patient-Centered**: Cooperation should improve safety, empathy, and the quality of care.
    1. **Crucial Perspective**

The future of medicine is human + AI, not human vs. machine. When combined, they create a hybrid intelligence that can identify illness early, tailor treatment, and produce superior results—all while maintaining the empathy, morality, and logic that are unique to humans.

2.11. Conclusion: Developing Confidence in the AI Physician

Artificial intelligence is a reality in healthcare today, not just a futuristic idea. AI is transforming medicine, from identifying minute nodules in the lungs to anticipating consequences from diabetes and deciphering intricate clinical notes.

However, the AI doctor's potential can only be fulfilled if institutions, professionals, and patients have faith in it.

Building trust requires openness, dependability, cooperation, and moral responsibility rather than naive faith.

1. **Precision and Dependability**

Performance is the first step towards trust. AI must continuously exhibit:

- Robust performance across populations and data kinds;
- Low false positives and negatives; and
- High sensitivity and specificity.

Confidence in AI suggestions is based on dependable outcomes that have been verified in practical contexts.

1. **Explainability and Transparency**

Clinicians will only have faith in AI if its logic makes sense:

- *Why was this nodule flagged by the AI?*
- *What made one diagnosis more important than another?*

Instead of depending on a "black box," explainable AI enables physicians to evaluate, confirm, and act confidently on recommendations.

1. **Human Supervision and Cooperation**

AI should support human doctors, not take their place. The collaboration between humans and AI guarantees:

- Context-sensitive and ethical decision-making.
- Protection from "weird mistakes" or AI blunders;
- Tailored care based on patient preferences and values.

When AI is used in conjunction with a doctor rather than in place of them, patients are more likely to trust it.

1. **Secure and Ethical Procedures**

Responsible AI deployment is also essential for trust:

- Patients must comprehend and provide their consent to AI-assisted care;
- Patient data must be kept private and safe;
- Bias must be actively discovered and minimized;
- Accountability must be transparent in the event of errors.

Clinicians and patients are more inclined to depend on AI when it upholds privacy, justice, and ethics.

1. **Ongoing Education and Development**

AI models get better with time, but only if mistakes, comments, and results are tracked.

When consumers observe:

- The AI learning from real-world instances;
- Constantly lowering errors and improving forecasts;
- Updates reflecting new medical knowledge.

Instead of being a static tool, it becomes a learning partner.

1. Crucial Perspective

Reliability, openness, ethical responsibility, and human oversight are the cornerstones of trust in the AI doctor. When these foundations are in place, *AI can improve medical practice by making treatment safer, quicker, and more accurate while retaining the empathy and judgment that only humans can offer.*

The hospital of the future will not be a place where humans and machines compete; rather, it will be a place where artificial intelligence and human intelligence collaborate, each enhancing the other, with the ultimate goal of improving each patient's health.

Chapter 3: AI Diagnostics: Identifying What People Miss

Overview

The core of medical practice is diagnosis. Treatment decisions, patient outcomes, and subsequent stages of care are all influenced by it. However, diagnostic errors continue to be one of the main sources of avoidable injury globally, despite the availability of contemporary techniques. AI has emerged as a radical solution: *a system that can analyse data at a scale that no person could ever accomplish, identify microscopic patterns, and investigate millions of cases.*

AI diagnostics aims to change medicine into a field where illnesses are detected earlier, more accurately, and more fairly. It is not just about technology.

3.1. The Change in Diagnosis

AI has completely changed the way diagnoses are produced, transforming what was once a laborious, manual, and error-prone procedure into a quicker, more intelligent, and more accurate medical workflow. Machine learning systems that have been trained on millions of clinical cases are at the core of this revolution, enabling AI to recognize patterns significantly more accurately than humans.

AI is now able to evaluate medical imaging, including MRIs, CT scans, ultrasounds, and X-rays, with a level of sensitivity that can identify anomalies before more conventional techniques can. It takes only a few seconds to detect microscopic lung nodules, micro-tumours, early stroke symptoms, or modest heart irregularities. AI tools can provide immediate preliminary assessments, speeding up therapy and enhancing results, rather than waiting hours or days for experts to evaluate scans.

Beyond imaging, AI simultaneously examines lab data, symptoms, genetic markers, and patient history—something that even the most skilled physicians are unable to do quickly. This comprehensive approach results in more precise and customized diagnostic forecasts. *AI serves as a "digital second opinion" in many hospitals, lowering misdiagnosis, drawing attention to diseases that are often neglected, and providing physicians with evidence-based insights.*

In the end, *AI's impact on diagnosis will empower physicians rather than replace them.* AI is transforming diagnostic medicine into a quicker, safer, and more data-driven field by detecting illnesses early, reducing human error, and offering real-time analysis.

3.2. Case Study: Early Breast Cancer Detection

One of the diseases where AI has had the most significant, life-saving effect is breast cancer. Early-stage cancers, particularly micro-calcifications, have historically been difficult to detect on mammograms because they show up as small, pale clusters that even skilled radiologists can miss. Patients are frequently diagnosed only after the tumour has grown, spread, or become more challenging to treat as a result of missing these early indicators.

This story has been altered by AI.

Hospitals used deep-learning mammography systems trained on millions of breast pictures in a significant study. The AI system identified minute irregularities in a 42-year-old woman's scan during screening—specks so tiny that they were almost undetectable to the human eye. The scan was deemed normal in the first radiological report, but the AI insisted on a high-risk score, necessitating a second assessment.

One of the earliest and most curable types of breast cancer, *Ductal Carcinoma in Situ* (DCIS), was verified by a follow-up biopsy. The patient only needed a minimally invasive operation instead of complete chemotherapy or a mastectomy because the cancer was found at this extremely early stage. Her prognosis was good, she recovered quickly, and her life expectancy remained the same.

Similar results are being reported all across the world. Mammography with AI assistance:

- By identifying early malignancies that are frequently overlooked, it lowers false negatives.
- By serving as a digital co-pilot, it increases radiologist accuracy.
- Reduces reading time, enabling earlier interventions and more

screens.

- Raises survival rates since better results are closely correlated with early detection.

By identifying tumours before they develop, spread, or even become apparent to human interpretation, this instance demonstrates how AI is not just aiding diagnostics but also saving lives.

3.3. AI in Radiology: The Revolution of the "Second Pair of Eyes"

AI, which is currently considered by many to be the second set of eyes that every radiologist needs, is at the core of the historic shift that radiology is going through. Radiologists have had to deal with heavy workloads, complicated imaging data, and the ongoing possibility of human mistake for decades. AI has taken over to improve their accuracy, speed, and confidence rather than to replace them.

Current AI systems use superhuman pattern recognition to evaluate medical images, including X-rays, CT scans, MRIs, and PET scans. These algorithms, which have been trained on millions of annotated photos, are able to identify irregularities that are too subtle or uncommon for even seasoned experts to regularly identify. *AI quickly detects critical clues, such as the faint shadow of a lung nodule, early ischemia alterations in a stroke patient, or micro-fractures concealed in dense tissue.*

Several innovations are brought about by this "AI co-pilot":

- **Error Reduction**: AI detects anomalies that radiologists might overlook because of complexity or weariness.
- **Consistency:** There is no variance or oversight; the same degree of inspection is applied consistently.
- **Speed:** AI can digest scans in seconds, allowing for quick triage in crises, whereas radiologists normally need minutes to interpret them.
- **Decision** support: It delivers evidence-based insights, evaluates the likelihood of disease, and indicates suspicious areas.

In reality, radiologists now use AI as a safety measure rather than a substitute, much like airplanes use autopilot. AI evaluates a scan first, then the radiologist reviews it with the use of Heatmaps, predicted scores, and highlighted risk zones. Diagnostic confidence is significantly increased by this cooperative model.

This is the true revolution: even in institutions that are overworked or understaffed, AI guarantees that every patient's scan is examined with expert-level attention. Radiologists become more proficient, accurate, and empowered, enabling them to diagnose patients more quickly while upholding the highest standards of care.

3.4. AI and Dermatology: Using a Smartphone to Diagnose Skin Cancer

AI has made the smartphone one of the most potent dermatology tools ever made, enabling regular people to detect skin cancer early and outside of a clinic. Skin cancer, especially melanoma, is highly treatable when diagnosed early. Access has always been a problem since many patients wait to see a dermatologist until the lesion has worsened, changed shape, or started to spread.

This issue is being resolved by AI.

Deep learning algorithms that have been trained on millions of dermatoscopic and clinical skin pictures are used in today's dermatology AI applications. The algorithm evaluates the mole's shape, asymmetry, boundaries, colour patterns, and texture using only a smartphone camera—the same parameters used by dermatologists, but with unparalleled computational accuracy.

This is an example of a typical situation:

> *A little dark spot appears on the shoulder of a 29-year-old male. It doesn't appear concerning enough to warrant a trip to the hospital. He takes a picture with an AI-powered dermatological app. The AI determines a high-risk level and suggests an immediate evaluation in a matter of seconds. He goes to a clinic where a dermatologist does a biopsy because he is worried.*
>
> *Early-stage melanoma, detected before it spread, was the diagnosis.*

His life might have been saved by a simple phone snap.

AI-driven dermatology has a number of transformative benefits:

- **Early Detection Anywhere:** No appointment with a specialist is required.
- **Quick Evaluation**: Results show up in a matter of seconds.
- **Greater Access**: Particularly for rural areas where dermatologists are scarce.
- **Greater Accuracy:** According to certain studies, AI's detection accuracy is on par with or higher than that of experts.
- **Continuous Monitoring:** Using weekly pictures, patients can monitor changes in moles over time.

Instead of taking the place of dermatologists, AI serves as a digital scout, identifying problematic lesions long before most people would consider getting medical attention. The combination of AI and smartphone technologies is changing the diagnosis of skin cancer from a late-stage finding to an early, avoidable action.

3.5. AI in Pathology: Future Microscopes

The foundation of medical diagnosis has always been pathology, the science of examining tissues and cells under a microscope. However, it continues to be one of the most labour-intensive and laborious specialty. Every day, a single pathologist might examine hundreds of slides with thousands of cells on them, looking for minute patterns that might point to illness, cancer, or infection. By turning the microscope into an intelligent, digital diagnostic assistant, AI is revolutionizing this procedure.

Pathology systems with AI capabilities today scan entire tissue slides and perform pixel-by-pixel analysis. These technologies detect anomalies such aberrant cell shapes, peculiar staining patterns, structural distortions, and concealed groupings of cancerous cells—sometimes before they are visually apparent to experts—instead of depending exclusively on the human sight.

An example of a significant innovation is the use of AI for digital pathology analysis in a hospital. A very tiny clump of abnormal cells that seemed nearly normal to the unaided eye was detected by the AI system during a regular breast biopsy screening. AI flagged it as "suspicious," but the first human assessment overlooked it.

Early invasive cancer, which is found at a stage when treatment is much more effective and less distressing for the patient, was confirmed by a second evaluation.

AI-driven pathology is bringing about a number of developments:

- **Superhuman Detail Detection**: AI looks at every pixel without becoming tired or side-tracked.
- **Significant Time Savings**: minutes instead of hours of human slide review.
- **Standardization**: uniform interpretation throughout hospitals and geographical areas.

- **Digital Workflows**: slides can be rapidly saved, examined, compared, and shared.
- **Increased Precision**—AI serves as a safeguard against overlooked early malignancies or minute alterations.

In many respects, AI is becoming into the new microscope—a tool that supplements rather than replaces the pathologist's skills. AI technologies that provide unparalleled accuracy, consistency, and speed to one of medicine's most crucial diagnostic domains will assist humans in making final decisions in the hybrid future of pathology.

3.6. Cardiovascular Diagnosis: Anticipating Heart Attacks Before They Occur

Heart attacks are frequently the earliest warning symptom of cardiovascular disease, which continues to be the leading cause of mortality worldwide. *The tiny early signs that a patient is on the verge of a catastrophic cardiac event can be missed by conventional diagnostic methods like ECGs, stress tests, or routine checks.* This is being altered by AI, which is altering cardiology from reaction to prediction.

Large volumes of cardiovascular data, including ECG patterns, heart rate variability, imaging scans, cholesterol levels, genetic markers, lifestyle information, and even wearable device readings, are analysed by contemporary AI systems using deep learning. Microscopic risk signs that human clinicians frequently miss are picked up by them.

This change is demonstrated with a compelling real-world example:

> *An AI system employed in a cardiac clinic identified a 54-year-old patient as high risk despite having "normal" ECG values and no significant symptoms. In his ECG waveform, the AI found micro-patterns that are imperceptible to the human eye and are associated with early-stage cardiomyopathy. Doctors found that he had serious, undetected coronary artery disease after more testing. He received prompt treatment because this was discovered early, averting what would have been a deadly heart attack in a matter of months.*

Cardiology is being revolutionized by this predictive potential in a number of ways:

- **AI-enhanced ECGs**: Before they manifest clinical symptoms, algorithms detect early ischemia, arrhythmias, and structural heart issues.

- **AI-Powered Cardiac Imaging**: AI accurately interprets MRIs, CT angiograms, and echocardiograms to measure heart function and identify plaque vulnerability.
- **Wearables with AI monitoring**: Smart watches can now identify irregular heart rhythms, such as atrial fibrillation, and provide real-time alarms well in advance of any problems.
- **Risk Prediction Models**: AI algorithms predict a patient's 1-year, 5-year, or 10-year risk of a cardiac event by combining lifestyle and clinical data.

As a result, there is a paradigm shift: AI enables medical professionals to completely avoid heart attacks rather than treat them after they occur. Predictive, individualized, and proactive cardiovascular diagnosis is saving lives long before symptoms manifest.

3.7. AI in Ophthalmology: Large-Scale Blindness Prevention

One of the most serious yet avoidable global health issues is blindness. Patients with conditions like diabetic retinopathy, glaucoma, macular degeneration, and cataracts frequently have no symptoms until they have started to lose their vision. By then, treatment is more difficult, results are worse, and the harm is frequently irreversible.

This narrative is being rewritten by AI, which makes population-scale early detection possible.

AI systems used in modern ophthalmology analyse retinal scans with remarkable accuracy, identifying minute alterations in blood vessels, nerve fibres, and retinal layers long before human experts can. By detecting microscopic micro-aneurysms and mild swelling, for instance, these devices can identify early diabetic retinopathy—much earlier than regular eye exams usually reveal.

An important example is the use of AI-powered retinal scanners in rural clinics as part of a nationwide diabetes screening program:

> *A routine visit was made by a 36-year-old lady with poorly controlled diabetes. The AI system examined her retinal pictures right away and identified early-stage diabetic retinopathy, despite the fact that she had no symptoms and probably would not have seen a specialist. Her vision was fully intact after she was treated with laser therapy and quickly referred.*

She would have been blind in a matter of years if it weren't for AI. AI is significantly changing ophthalmology in a number of ways.

- **Mass Screening in Minutes:** Even in areas without ophthalmologists, AI systems are able to analyse thousands of retinal scans every day.

- **Unmatched Accuracy:** AI may sometimes detect diabetic retinopathy and other eye conditions just as well as or better than specialists.
- **Reaching Underserved Communities**: In remote and low-resource environments, portable AI retinal scanners provide top-notch diagnosis.
- **Early Intervention:** Blindness rates are significantly decreased when illness is identified at its earliest, most treatable stage.
- **Continuous Monitoring**: With no effort on the part of the patient, AI-integrated devices provide continuous surveillance of illness progression.

As a result, blindness is no longer a fate that millions of people must endure. AI enables healthcare systems to identify eye disease early, treat it quickly, and preserve the gift of sight—at scale, effectively, and with previously unheard-of precision.

3.8. Predictive Diagnostics: Illness Before It Occurs

The potential of AI in medicine to anticipate illness before it emerges clinically is one of its most revolutionary promises. Conventional diagnostics are reactive; medical professionals diagnose disease only after symptoms manifest or testing verify pathology. This paradigm is reversed by AI, which moves healthcare from reaction to prevention.

AI's capacity to evaluate large, complicated datasets, including genetic data, lab results, imaging data, lifestyle variables, wearable device readings, and electronic health records, is essential to predictive diagnosis. AI can predict a person's risk of developing diseases like diabetes, cancer, cardiovascular disease, or neurological disorders years in advance by spotting minute patterns and correlations that are imperceptible to the human eye.

As a real-world example:

> *An AI predictive model processes a patient's routine check-up data, including blood pressure, cholesterol, family history, and wearable heart rate trends. Despite the fact that present blood sugar levels are normal, the algorithm determines a high likelihood of getting type 2 diabetes during the following five years. Equipped with this knowledge, medical professionals develop a customized preventative strategy that includes medicine, exercise, and food. The patient's risk of developing a full-blown illness and its complications is decreased with early intervention.*

Among the main advantages of predictive diagnostics are:

- **Early Intervention**: Rather than treating symptoms later, it prevents the start of the disease.

- **Customized healthcare:** Preventive measures based on each patient's unique risk profile.
- **Resource Optimization**: Reduces needless testing by concentrating medical care on high-risk patients.
- **Population Health Management**: Makes it possible for healthcare systems to effectively identify and track at-risk populations.
- **Continuous Learning**: As more patient data is gathered, AI models get better over time, increasing prediction accuracy.

By shifting from reactive care to proactive, precision prevention—where diseases are foreseen, treated, and frequently completely avoided—predictive diagnostics offers a paradigm leap in medicine that will change how we live longer, healthier lives.

3.9. AI in Lab Medicine: More Intelligent Examinations, Quicker Outcomes

Accurate analysis of blood, urine, tissue, and other biological samples is essential to laboratory medicine, which is the foundation of diagnosis and treatment. Lab testing has historically been laborious, prone to human error, and limited in the intricacy of patterns it can identify. All of that is changing as AI makes lab medicine more accurate, quicker, and intelligent.

Massive amounts of lab data may be analysed nearly quickly by AI algorithms, which can identify minute abnormalities that point to illness, infection, or metabolic imbalance before conventional criteria are exceeded. By evaluating normal blood tests, vital signs, and patient history, for example, AI can predict the start of sepsis and notify physicians hours or even days ahead of time compared to traditional techniques.

Important uses consist of:

- **Automated Sample Analysis:** With little human participation, AI-powered devices can process thousands of samples per hour, cutting down on errors and turnaround time.
- **Pattern Recognition**: By identifying intricate connections between biomarkers, test results, and patient history, early-stage diseases can be better understood.
- **Predictive Testing**: AI models can suggest more focused tests based on minute irregularities found, guaranteeing that no important data is overlooked.
- **Quality Control:** AI continuously analyses laboratory procedures, identifying discrepancies or equipment malfunctions instantly.
- **Personalized Diagnostics:** AI can provide patient-specific

diagnostic insights by integrating test results with genomes and lifestyle data.

A real-world example:

An AI system in a medical lab detected a patient's combination of abnormal blood cell patterns and mild increases of liver enzymes. This led to more testing, which revealed early-stage liver fibrosis—diagnosed before to the onset of symptoms, enabling rapid treatment and halting the development of cirrhosis.

AI is making laboratory medicine a proactive, high-precision discipline by speeding up workflows, improving accuracy, and identifying hidden trends. This is transforming routine tests into effective instruments for early intervention and improved patient outcomes.

3.10. How AI Lowers Diagnostic Mistakes

In medicine, diagnostic errors continue to be a significant problem that can lead to treatment delays, poor management, and avoidable patient harm. Under pressure, even the most experienced medical professionals may fail to notice subtle symptoms, neglect uncommon illnesses, or make poor decisions. AI is becoming a vital ally in lowering these mistakes, serving as a force multiplier and safety net for human expertise.

AI lowers diagnostic mistakes in key ways:

1. **Pattern Recognition beyond Human Capabilities**: AI examines enormous datasets, including test results, medical imaging, and patient histories, and finds trends or abnormalities that people might miss. For instance, AI can identify minute cellular alterations in pathology or subtle lesions in radiography early.
2. **Consistency and Standardization:** AI is not subject to cognitive bias or tiredness like humans are. In order to minimize variability and guarantee uniform diagnostic quality across patients and facilities, every scan, slide, or test is examined with the same level of rigor.
3. **Decision Support and Risk Prioritization**: AI highlights high-risk regions for further investigation by giving doctors risk rankings, Heatmaps, and evidence-based recommendations. This serves as a "second opinion," assisting medical professionals in concentrating on the most important discoveries.
4. **Early Identification of Rare Conditions**: Atypical appearances or rare diseases may elude early diagnosis. AI that has been trained on millions of cases can identify odd trends

that could lead to additional research, avoiding missed or delayed diagnosis.

5. **Error input Loops:** AI systems are always learning from new instances, results, and input from clinicians. Over time, this repeated learning decreases recurrent errors in comparable clinical circumstances and increases accuracy.

An example in action:

According to a study, using AI in radiology lowered the number of lung cancer cases that were missed by 20% by identifying nodules that human radiologists had missed. Similar to this, early-stage tumours that were initially overlooked during regular examination were found in pathology thanks to AI-assisted slide analysis.

Diagram: How an AI Learns to Detect Lung Cancer

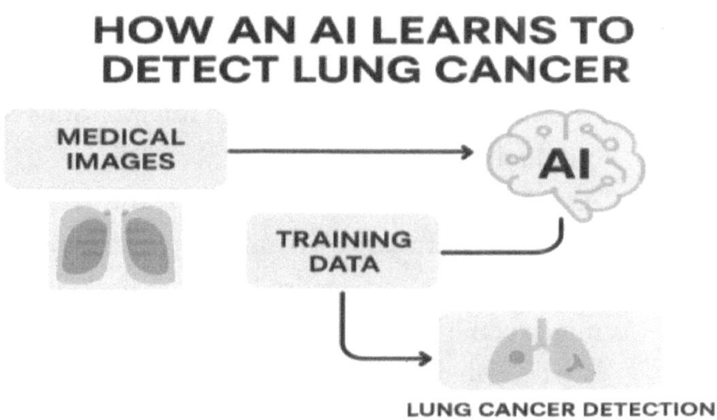

Figure 5: How an AI Learns to Detect Lung Cancer

AI dramatically lowers diagnostic errors by serving as a watchful, diligent, and evidence-based companion. This improves patient safety, boosts clinical confidence, and ultimately saves lives.

3.11. Clinical Difficulties: When AI Makes an Error

AI has transformed diagnoses, but it is not perfect. Algorithmic constraints, skewed training data, or unforeseen patient characteristics can all lead to errors. To properly incorporate AI into clinical practice, it is crucial to recognize these risks.

Important issues when AI commits errors:

1. **Representation Gaps and Data Bias:** The quality of AI models depends on the quality of the data used to train them. The AI may misdiagnose populations if training datasets lack diversity, for as by underrepresenting particular age groups, races, or uncommon ailments. A skin cancer detection AI that was mostly trained on lighter skin tones, for instance, would perform poorly on darker skin.
2. **Overreliance by Clinicians:** Physicians may ignore contradicting clinical indicators in favour of AI suggestions. Missed diagnoses or postponed interventions may result from blind faith in AI.
3. **Ambiguous or Confounding Data:** AI algorithms may become confused by complicated situations, overlapping conditions, or low-quality images. False positives or negatives might come from a noisy ECG, fuzzy imaging, or incorrectly labelled lab data.
4. **Lack of Explainability:** A lot of AI models, particularly deep learning systems, function as "black boxes," making predictions without providing a clear explanation. It could be difficult for clinicians to comprehend why the AI made a particular conclusion, which would complicate accountability and decision-making.
5. **Technical and System Errors:** Inaccurate outputs or delayed

important alarms might result from device failures, software faults, or integration problems with hospital information systems.

Example in Practice:

Due to visual distortions brought on by dim lighting, an AI system in a diabetic retinopathy screening program incorrectly identified the retinal scans of many individuals. These mistakes show the danger of relying too much on AI alone, even though they were discovered during human review.

Mitigation strategies include:

- Constantly validate and retrain models using a variety of real-world data;
- Always utilize AI as a decision-support tool, not as a substitute for physician judgment.
- Keep human monitoring in place for issues that are unclear or have significant consequences.
- Create AI algorithms that can be explained so that medical professionals can comprehend and challenge forecasts.

Although AI has revolutionary potential, its mistakes serve as a reminder that human knowledge, discretion, and attention to detail are still necessary for safe and efficient patient care.

3.12. Legal and Ethical Issues with AI Diagnostics

Deep ethical and legal concerns are raised by the growing integration of AI in medical diagnosis. AI can improve speed, accuracy, and accessibility, but it also calls into question established standards of patient autonomy, privacy, and accountability. For deployment to be both safe and equitable, these factors must be taken into account.

Important Ethical Points to Remember:

1. **Responsibility and Accountability**: It is unclear who is morally and legally accountable when an AI system misdiagnoses a patient: the hospital, the developer, or the treating physician. Liability in circumstances of injury must be defined using precise frameworks.

2. **Bias and Fairness:** If AI systems are trained on non-representative datasets, they may reinforce or magnify pre-existing biases. This could result in systemic discrimination, unequal treatment, or incorrect diagnosis in underrepresented groups.

3. **Explainability and Transparency:** Clinicians and patients need to know how AI arrives at its judgments. "Black-box" models that are unable to justify a choice run the risk of eroding informed consent and confidence.

4. **Informed Consent:** Patients should be informed about the possible dangers and restrictions associated with using AI technologies for diagnosis and treatment planning. The potential for AI inaccuracy and the integration of human oversight should be covered in consent.

5. **Data Security and Privacy:** AI depends on a lot of private patient information. To safeguard patients from breaches or misuse, it is essential to ensure secure storage, appropriate data exchange, and compliance with privacy requirements (such as HIPAA or GDPR).

Important legal considerations include:

- **Regulatory Approval**: To guarantee safety and effectiveness, AI diagnostic tools must adhere to criteria defined by medical regulatory organizations (such as the FDA and EMA).
- **Intellectual Property**: Concerns are raised about who owns insights produced by AI and if diagnostic recommendations belong to AI developers or physicians.
- **Liability in Malpractice**: When AI involvement challenges standard malpractice findings, courts and medical boards must address these situations.

An example in action:

Hospitals must deal with the ethical and legal ramifications if an AI system determines a patient is cancer-free yet misses early-stage disease, delaying treatment: Was it careless of the clinician to put their faith in the AI? Does the AI developer have to take accountability? Policies that define these responsibilities are still being developed.

In the end, ethical and legal supervision guarantees that AI in diagnostics benefits patients in a fair and safe manner. In addition to precise medicine, the objective is trustworthy medicine, where technical advancement is in line with human values, accountability, and fairness.

3.13. The Future: Personalized, Instantaneous, and Anywhere Diagnostics

AI is transforming medical diagnostics into what was previously considered science fiction: instantaneous, omnipresent, and individualized treatment. Innovations in cloud computing, wearable technology, and machine learning are coming together to deliver diagnostics to patients at any time and from any location.

Important aspects of this future include:

1. **Quick Diagnostics:** Real-time analysis of patient data, including imaging, lab results, vitals, and genetic markers, will be done by AI-powered devices. Immediate diagnostic insights from a smartphone, smart watch, or portable scanner could eliminate the need for numerous appointments and lengthy wait times.
2. **Diagnostics All Around**: AI tools that previously required specialized equipment and trained professionals will be available to households, mobile health units, and rural clinics. By enabling early detection and intervention for traditionally marginalized communities, this democratizes healthcare.
3. **Customized Healthcare:** AI will combine personal genetics, medical history, lifestyle information, and environmental factors to deliver individualized diagnoses. Customized risk assessments, preventive measures, and treatment recommendations will maximize results and reduce needless interventions.
4. **Predictive and Preventive Focus:** AI will foresee potential health hazards in addition to identifying current problems. Wearable sensors and home-based diagnostics will enable

ongoing monitoring, which will change medical treatment from reactive to proactive by enabling intervention before symptoms manifest.

5. **Smooth Integration with Care:** AI diagnostics will be integrated into electronic health records and care platforms, allowing for coordinated follow-up care, automatic alarms, and real-time communication with healthcare professionals.

An example in action:

Consider a patient who has a history of heart disease in their family. AI examines blood pressure patterns and exercise data, while a smart watch continuously tracks heart rhythms. Before any clinical signs appear, the system finds early arrhythmia, notifies the patient and physician, and suggests tailored interventions.

A world where diagnoses are quick, available, and customized—empowering patients, lowering the burden of disease, and establishing a truly preventative healthcare paradigm—is promised by the convergence of AI, digital health, and personalized medicine.

A new era of medicine is emerging, one that meets patients where they are, foresees issues before they arise, and provides individualized therapy.

3.14. Conclusion the Revolution in AI Diagnostics Has Already Started

The revolution in AI diagnostics is already under way; it has transcended theory and pilot research. *AI is revolutionizing the detection, interpretation, and treatment of diseases in a variety of fields, including radiology, pathology, cardiology, dermatology, ophthalmology, and laboratory medicine.*

Important conclusions:

- **Accuracy and Speed:** AI improves diagnostic accuracy, lowers human error, and speeds up decision-making across a variety of medical disciplines.
- **Early Detection:** It is now feasible to detect life-threatening illnesses including cancer, heart disease, and retinal impairment at much earlier stages than in the past.
- **Accessibility:** AI democratizes healthcare by bringing expert-level diagnostics to underfunded clinics, remote locations, and even personal devices.
- **Predictive Power:** AI provides proactive, preventive, and individualized care by anticipating sickness rather than merely detecting it.
- **Human-AI Collaboration**: AI serves as a digital co-pilot, enhancing human judgment and facilitating safer, more intelligent medical judgments rather than taking the place of physicians.

There are still issues, such as moral conundrums, legal responsibility, data privacy, and sporadic algorithmic mistakes, but they are being resolved by careful planning, legislation, and human monitoring.

A paradigm shift is represented by the AI diagnostic revolution: *medicine is now predictive, accurate, and individualized rather than merely reactive.* Clinicians are equipped with previously unthinkable insights, and patients are receiving faster, safer, and more precise care.

Globally, hospitals, clinics, and research facilities are already undergoing the change. One thing is certain as AI develops further: *the era of more intelligent, quicker, and easily available diagnostics is here, and it's just getting started.*

Chapter 4: AI-Powered Therapy: From Procedures to Accurate Recovery

Overview: From Intelligent Care to One-Size-Fits-All

Standardized protocols, universal pharmaceutical dosages, manual monitoring, and episodic intervention were the hallmarks of clinical treatment for decades. These techniques produced blind spots even though they worked well in a time when data and processing capacity were few. Healthcare systems found it difficult to get past "one-size-fits-all" methods; patients reacted differently to treatments; and consequences were discovered too late.

Standardized clinical procedures have been the mainstay of medical care for many years. The recommended drug or therapy frequently adhered to the same guidelines regardless of the patient's weight (50 or 120 kg), level of activity, or number of comorbidities. Although this method saved lives, it also resulted in treatment failures, unpleasant responses, inefficiencies, and preventable fatalities.

This paradigm is changing nowadays.

A new era of dynamic, intelligent, personalized, and predictive treatment has been ushered in by artificial intelligence (AI). AI is making therapy a constantly evolving process, from intelligent monitoring in intensive care units to AI-guided surgical robots and real-time medication dosage modifications. The essence of healing is being redefined by AI, as this chapter examines.

Precision healing, *where treatments are continuously modified based on real-time patient data*, represents a drastic departure from population-based medicine with AI-driven treatment. AI predicts, monitors, and modifies treatment routes with amazing accuracy, saving clinicians from speculating about a patient's potential response.

Diagram: AI Powered Therapy

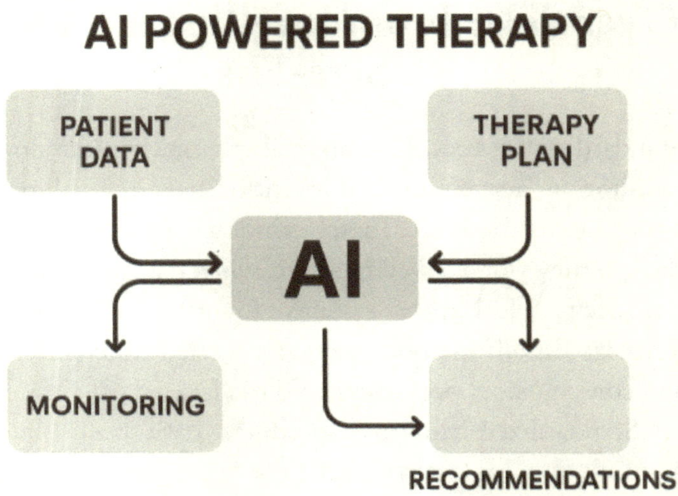

Figure 6: AI Powered Therapy

This change is not theoretical; it is currently taking place in hospitals. Operating AI is bringing about a future in which:

- Medicine dosages self-adjust;
- Robotic precision treatment is used in operating rooms and homes worldwide.
- The effects are reduced.
- Healing becomes proactive rather than reactive; therapies are customized to each patient's biology.

Greetings from the precision healing era.

4.1. Customized Treatment Plans Driven by AI

Conventional treatment plans adhere to evidence-based averages from extensive clinical trials. By examining enormous multi-dimensional datasets, such as genetic profiles, medical histories, and lifestyle factors, AI challenges this:

- Reaction to previous therapies;
- Environmental factors.

AI can create individualized treatment regimens that are tailored to each patient using machine learning models. Due to differences in their bodies, behaviours, and risks, two people with the same condition may have completely different treatment regimens.

Example: Customized Oncology

The potential of AI customisation is demonstrated by cancer treatment. Tumour genetics can be analysed by AI systems to identify probable mutations, expected resistance patterns, and the most effective chemotherapy. Higher success rates and decreased toxicity result from this.

AI-driven tailoring improves success rates, decreases trial-and-error treatment, and speeds up recovery.

4.2. AI's Development in Therapy

The introduction of AI into medicine reflects the larger digital revolution in healthcare:

Phase 1: Systems Based on Rules (1990s–2000s)

Strict IF-THEN logic was the foundation of early AI tools. They lacked adaptability yet encouraged decision-making. These systems might adhere to procedures, but they wouldn't adjust to the individuality of each patient.

Phase 2: Algorithms for Prediction (2010–2020)

Systems were able to learn from data thanks to machine learning. Proactive treatment was made possible by models that started forecasting difficulties, medication reactions, and illness progression.

Phase 3: Adaptive Treatment in Real Time (2020–Present)

The development of real-time, patient-specific, continually adapting AI treatment systems was made possible by advances in deep learning, computer vision, natural language processing, and sensor integration.

Phase 4: Emerging Autonomous AI Treatment Ecosystems

AI robots, dosing engines, digital twins, and remote-care platforms are examples of integrated networks of autonomous systems that will manage treatment as a cohesive, intelligent workflow in the future.

Diagram: Advances in AI in Medicine

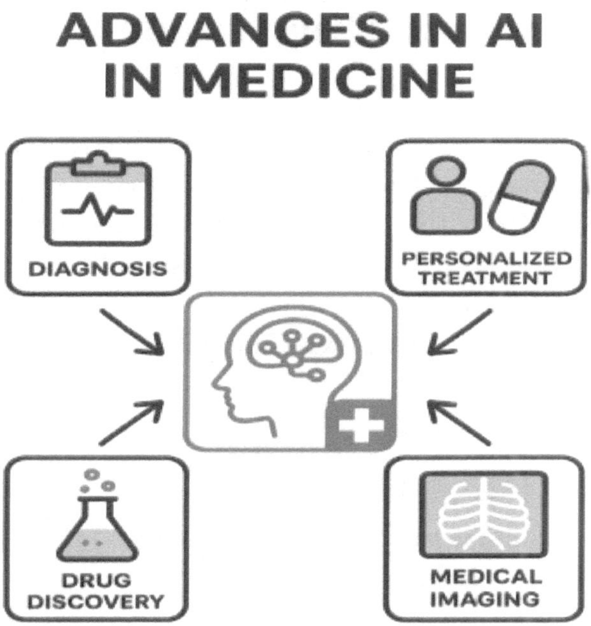

Figure 7: Advances in AI in Medicine

4.3. AI in Medication Administration and Drug Dosing

One of the most difficult problems in medicine is drug dosage. Little changes in dosage can make the difference between toxicity and therapeutic effect. By modifying medications based on real-time physiological data, lab results, and patient monitoring devices, AI-driven dosage algorithms are transforming drug management.

Predictive models

Case Study: AI Adapting Cancer Therapy to a Patient's Genetics

Patient's Background:

Maria, a 52-year-old lady, received a stage II breast cancer diagnosis. In the past, traditional chemotherapy procedures were used for treatment, which frequently had serious side effects and varied effectiveness. But Maria's facility incorporates precision oncology powered by AI into its treatment plan.

Step 1: Genomic Analysis

- Full genome sequencing is performed on Maria's tumour sample.
- To find useful targets, AI examines gene expression patterns, biological pathways, and mutations.
- An unusual mutation in the HER2 gene is detected by the system, indicating receptivity to a targeted therapy that is not usually recommended in conventional treatment protocols.

Step 2: Treatment Suggestion

- Maria's tumour profile is compared to thousands of cancer cases worldwide, clinical trials, and medication databases by the AI platform.
- To optimize effectiveness and reduce toxicity, it suggests a combination of targeted HER2 treatment with a lower-dose chemotherapy regimen.
- Based on Maria's genetic and metabolic profile, the AI also forecasts possible adverse consequences.

Step 3: Adaptation and Dynamic Monitoring

- Maria wears a non-invasive biosensor that monitors her vital signs, tumour indicators, and medication response during her treatment.
- By continuously analysing the data, the AI system finds early indicators of negative responses or decreased medication efficacy. The AI recommends a small dosage change to maximize drug delivery after two treatment cycles, avoiding needless side effects while preserving tumour suppression.

Step 4: Outcome and Impact

- Compared to other chemotherapy patients, Maria has less adverse effects.
- Tumour indicators rapidly fall, and imaging reveals considerable tumour shrinkage.
- The individualized, AI-guided strategy raises the likelihood of long-term remission and reduces the length of treatment.

Important Lessons:

1. **Precision over Protocols**: AI leverages Maria's genetic data to move beyond one-size-fits-all therapy.

2. **Predictive Side Effect Management**: Patients' quality of life is enhanced by anticipating toxicities.
3. **Adaptive therapy:** Real-time modifications made possible by ongoing monitoring make treatment safer and more successful.
4. **Global Knowledge Integration**: AI uses global cancer data to offer innovative therapy suggestions.

In conclusion, Maria's case serves as an example of how AI is changing oncology from strict treatment regimens to dynamic, genetics-driven precision medicine. Such AI-guided procedures will become more and more important in the future of cancer therapy, providing patients with hope for improved results and reduced burdens.

4.4. AI in the Management of Chronic Illnesses: Constant Modification, Constant Recovery

Chronic conditions like diabetes, high blood pressure, heart failure, and COPD necessitate ongoing care and frequent treatment modifications. In the past, this responsibility was placed on patients and physicians, who relied more on planned visits than on ongoing understanding.

AI completely alters the model.

Important Changes

- **Constant Monitoring:** Wearables record blood pressure, heart rate variability, oxygen saturation, glucose, and more. These signals are instantly interpreted by AI.
- **Predictive Intervention**: AI predicts risk hours or days ahead of time rather than responding to catastrophes.
- **Medication Optimization:** Without waiting for symptoms, AI modifies the use of insulin, inhalers, antihypertensive, or heart failure drugs.

Example: AI in Diabetes Management:

Insulin pumps powered by AI now act as automated pancreases, anticipating changes in blood sugar levels minutes in advance, modifying insulin administration, and averting hypoglycaemia.

Case Study: Intelligent Heart Failure Monitoring

Early detection of fluid retention patterns is made possible by remote sensors and AI algorithms. Hospitals that use these systems claim lower death rates, faster symptom stabilization, and a 30–50% decrease in hospital readmissions.

AI transforms the treatment of chronic illnesses from episodic to ongoing.

4.5. Robotic Surgery Powered by AI: Precision beyond Human Capability

Robotic surgery is now a common practice at top hospitals across the globe; it is no longer science fantasy.

Robotic surgery is improved by AI by providing:

1. **Superhuman Accuracy:** Robotic arms remove vibrations, enabling sub-millimetre accuracy.

2. Systems of Intelligent Guidance

AI models evaluate CT/MRI pictures, aiding robots:

- Map tissue borders;
- Steer clear of important structures;
- Forecast surgical complications;
- Give immediate feedback.

3. Capabilities That Are Semi-Autonomous: AI lessens surgeon fatigue by helping in suturing, cutting, coagulation, and endoscope positioning.

4. Personalisation: Pre-operative "digital twin" simulations optimize results by enabling surgeons to virtually practice procedures.

Example: AI-Guided Prostate Surgery

Robotic technologies preserve sexual and urine function by reducing nerve injury and improving cancer margin clearing.

Surgical perfection is redefined by AI-enhanced robotics.

4.6. AI in Radiation Therapy: Accurately Targeting Tumours at the Microscopic Level

Exquisite precision is necessary for radiation therapy. Healthy tissues could be harmed by even a millimetre of displacement.

AI improves radiation treatment by:

Automated Segmentation of Tumours

Compared to human radiologists, deep learning models identify tumour boundaries on imaging more quickly and reliably.

Adaptive Radiation Therapy

Every day, AI modifies treatment regimens in response to tumour shrinking, patient mobility, organ deformation, and biological reaction.

Algorithms for predictive toxicity modelling identify patients who are most likely to have adverse effects and modify dosages appropriately.

Case Study: Treatment for Lung Cancer

AI-powered devices have improved survival rates and decreased complications by reducing radiation exposure to the oesophagus and heart by more than 20%.

AI improves the accuracy, adaptability, and safety of radiation therapy.

4.7. AI in ICU Care: Preserving Lives Every Minute

The ICU has a lot of data and is time-sensitive. Monitors and equipment produce more than 1,000 data points every second for a single patient. This volume cannot be manually analysed by human clinicians, but AI can.

Important ICU Uses

Predicting cardiac arrest six to twelve hours ahead of time; detecting sepsis before symptoms manifest; real-time detection of ventilator problems; improving sedation and pain management; and controlling ventilator settings using AI-driven closed-loop systems.

Example: Early Identification of Sepsis

Compared to traditional scoring systems, AI models that analyse lab trends and vital signs can notify clinicians hours earlier, significantly increasing survival.

AI works as a round-the-clock co-clinician in the intensive care unit.

4.8. AI in Mental Health Care: Comprehending the Unseen

One of the most complicated areas of medicine is mental health since symptoms are subjective, sporadic, and impacted by a wide range of variables.

Where ambiguity once prevailed, AI delivers clarity.

Important Innovations

- **Emotion Recognition:** AI can identify stress, worry, or despair by analysing text patterns, voice, and face expressions.
- **Predictive Relapse Monitoring**: Data from smartphones and wearables can forecast psychotic or depressive episodes days in advance.
- **AI Therapists & Chat-Based CBT:** By providing prompt therapeutic assistance, digital assistants increase accessibility.
- **Customized Treatment Plans:** AI reduces trial-and-error by predicting which antidepressant a patient is most likely to respond to.

Example: Suicide Risk Prediction

In emergency rooms, machine learning algorithms have diagnosed high-risk patients with up to 90% accuracy, far surpassing human evaluation.

4.9. AI in Physiotherapy and Rehabilitation: Using Intelligence to Recover

The process of rehabilitation is drawn out and repeated. AI turns it into an intelligent, customized experience.

AI-Powered Methods

Robotic exoskeletons with real-time strength and resistance adjustments; computer vision systems that analyse patient movement to correct posture and gait; virtual and augmented reality platforms that offer immersive rehabilitation exercises; and predictive recovery modelling to determine the ideal frequency and duration of therapy

Case Study: Rehabilitation Following a Stroke

AI-powered exoskeletons assist patients regain their capacity to walk more quickly by detecting and amplifying micro-movements. According to studies:

- There is a 40% improvement in gait recovery,
- Less muscular fatigue, and
- More patient motivation.

Rehabilitation becomes data-driven, dynamic, and engaging.

4.10. AI-Reduced Treatment Errors: A New Safety Era

Globally, medical errors continue to be a major cause of death. AI dramatically lowers avoidable errors by:

Safety of Medications

- Identifying prescription errors;
- preventing incorrect dosages; and
- flagging drug interactions

Procedure Safety

- AI checklists during surgery;
- Automated alarms for missing stages; and
- Procedure safety.

Safety Monitoring

- Early detection of aberrant vital sign trends;
- Prevention of ICU alarm fatigue; and
- Detection of misconnected tubes or lines.

Workflow Safety and Documentation

- Automated reminders guarantee procedure adherence;
- AI transcription lowers charting errors

Throughout the whole course of treatment, AI serves as a real-time safety net.

4.11. Ethical Difficulties: The Impact of Machines on Life and Death

AI-driven therapy presents difficult moral dilemmas:

1. **Bias in Algorithms:** Certain groups may be treated unfairly by AI that was trained on a small amount of data.
2. **Privacy and Data Ownership:** *Who is the owner of treatment data from digital twins, wearables, and sensors?*
3. **Responsibility:** *Who is accountable—the developer, the physician, or the organization—when an AI system makes a choice that causes harm?*
4. **Autonomy of the Patient***: How do medical professionals make sure patients maintain control when algorithms are used to make decisions*?
5. **Transparency:** Informed consent is challenged by black-box models. Patients ought to understand the rationale behind a prescribed course of treatment.
   Capability and ethics must change together.

4.12. Completely Integrated AI Treatment Ecosystems: The Future Is Already Here

Instead of isolated AI tools, the next frontier will be fully integrated ecosystems where:

- AI makes diagnoses;
- AI chooses treatments;
- AI gives medication;
- AI monitors response;
- AI automatically modifies therapy;
- AI anticipates future complications; and
- Human clinicians supervise, validate, and step in when needed.

Digital twin patient simulators, AI-guided robots, real-time dosage engines, wearable biosensors, cloud-based monitoring systems, and hospital AI command centres are all included in the Connected Treatment Model.

Healthcare becomes intelligent, networked, and end-to-end optimized.

4.12.1. Practical Case Studies

Case Study 1: AI Preserves a Patient with Sepsis

There were no overt indications of decline in a 45-year-old patient who was admitted with pneumonia. One of the main causes of ICU deaths, early sepsis, was not detected by traditional monitoring techniques.

Six hours before clinical symptoms manifested, an AI early-warning system that analysed lab data, vital signs, and subtle physiological changes anticipated the onset of septic shock. Intervention was started right away:

- Targeted antibiotics; intensive fluid resuscitation;
- Support for vasopressors.
- The patient made a full recovery.
- The danger of death would have been very high in the absence of AI detection.

Case Study 2: Successful Customized Cancer Treatment

AI-driven genetic analysis was performed on a patient with breast cancer who did not respond well to conventional chemotherapy. An uncommon mutation that responded to a targeted treatment that isn't often recommended was found by the system.

Following a change in therapy:

- The tumour size significantly shrank,
- The side effects subsided, and
- The course of treatment was shortened.

AI personalization turned an unsuccessful course of treatment into a successful one.

Case Study #3: Reimagining Stroke Rehabilitation

An AI-powered rehabilitation system helped a stroke survivor who was having trouble moving about by analysing gait patterns, correcting movement faults, and adjusting training intensity.

Compared to patients receiving conventional physiotherapy:

- The patient recovered mobility 40% more quickly.

4.13. Two Crucial Lessons

- AI-driven dosing saves pharmaceutical errors;
- Robotic and AI-assisted surgery improves precision;
- Continuous monitoring transforms chronic care;
- Personalization improves results and minimizes adverse effects; and
- Ethical oversight is still crucial.

AI is reinventing treatment, not just supporting it.

Conclusion: Intelligence-Driven Therapy

Precision healing is replacing standardized protocols in medicine thanks to AI. AI-driven treatment improves results and revolutionizes patient care by employing real-time data, predictive analytics, and tailored interventions. Even more sophisticated systems with autonomous treatment management capabilities are anticipated in the future, resulting in safer and more efficient medical care.

AI is enhancing rather than replacing medical professionals, bringing us a new era of intelligence-driven healing. Treatment is changing from being reactive to proactive, generalized to individualized, episodic to continuous, and manual to autonomous.

Healing becomes safer, quicker, more accurate, and more compassionate in the era of AI-driven medical care.

This chapter emphasizes an important fact: *AI enhances medical care rather than just supporting it.* The transition from protocols to precision healing has started, and the intelligence we incorporate into medicine today will help patients in the future.

Chapter 5: AI in Diagnostics: Perceiving Things Humans Can't

Overview

Artificial intelligence is quickly emerging as the most significant diagnostic instrument in contemporary medicine. Human cognition—experience, intuition, and reasoning—was the foundation of healthcare for many years, but the proliferation of medical data has surpassed human capability. Massive streams of scans, lab results, genetic information, patient histories, symptoms, lifestyle records, wearable gadget feeds, and clinical guidelines must be interpreted by the modern physician. No human brain can process this volume in real time.

AI transforms everything.

These days, algorithms are capable of analysing millions of data points in a matter of seconds and finding patterns that even the most seasoned experts would miss. This chapter examines how AI is ushering in a new era of precision, speed, and predictive ability in diagnostic medicine.

5.1. Transitioning from Guesswork to Pattern Identification

Human intuition played a major role in medical diagnosis and therapy for ages. To diagnose illnesses and provide remedies, doctors employed clinical judgment, experience, and a combination of inference and guesswork. Although this method has saved many lives, it is intrinsically flawed since human cognition is prone to bias, inconsistency, and inaccuracy, particularly in complicated cases involving uncommon illnesses or overlapping symptoms.

This paradigm is changing due to artificial intelligence. AI is fundamentally good at pattern recognition, which is the capacity to find minute trends and correlations in enormous volumes of data that are invisible to the human eye. In a matter of seconds, millions of patient records, MRI scans, genomic sequences, and lab findings may be analysed by modern machine learning algorithms, which can spot trends that even seasoned experts might miss.

Consider the field of radiology. An AI system can identify minute changes in tissue density or shape—early warning indicators of disease—before symptoms ever appear, whereas a doctor might only notice noticeable anomalies on an MRI or X-ray. Similar to this, AI in oncology may evaluate intricate genomic data to determine which treatments a tumour is most likely to respond to, transforming care from general speculation to individualized precision medicine.

Instead of replacing human doctors, the transition from guesswork to pattern recognition enhances their skills. AI systems that offer probabilistic evaluations, reveal hidden trends, and recommend treatments based on past results are now helping doctors. Faster, more precise, and individualized medical decisions are made possible by this collaboration.

In the end, AI's aptitude for pattern recognition is transforming medicine from an art of intuition into a science of prediction, where data-driven insights lower uncertainty and enhance patient outcomes. What used to be a game of educated guesswork is evolving into a precise science driven by clever computers.

5.2. The New Stethoscope: AI-Powered Medical Imaging

The stethoscope represented a doctor's capacity to hear and understand the human body for many generations. AI-powered medical imaging is currently taking the place of the stethoscope, a vital instrument that enables physicians to see far beyond what is visible to the unaided eye.

Large volumes of visual data are produced by medical imaging, including MRIs, CT scans, ultrasounds, and X-rays, considerably more than any human radiologist could thoroughly examine. *These photos can be processed remarkably quickly and accurately by AI systems, especially those built on deep learning.* They enable early identification of diseases like cancer, heart disease, and neurological disorders by seeing minute patterns, anomalies, or changes over time.

Think about the discovery of lung cancer. Conventional scans could overlook tiny nodules that could grow into cancerous tumours. AI systems that have been trained on hundreds of imaging datasets are able to identify these nodules early, frequently even before symptoms manifest, providing patients with a critical therapeutic advantage. Similar to this, AI in cardiology can identify minute abnormalities in the structure or function of the heart and forecast possible heart attacks with previously unheard-of accuracy.

The effect goes beyond precision. AI-powered imaging eases the increasing strain on overworked radiologists, minimizes diagnostic delays, and standardizes interpretations across hospitals. Additionally, it makes expert-level analysis more accessible, allowing hospitals in underserved or distant areas to gain access to the same superior diagnostic insights as leading medical facilities.

However, *AI imaging is a tool, not a substitute for human skill, just like the stethoscope.* In order to understand AI results, place them in the context of a patient's overall health, and make complex treatment decisions, radiologists and doctors are still crucial. AI increases human capacity, transforming medical imaging from a reactive record of illness into a proactive tool of precision care.

To put it briefly, *AI-powered imaging is changing the way doctors "listen" to the body, moving medicine from observation to anticipation and from treating symptoms to intervening before illness manifests.*

5.3. Artificial Intelligence in Lab Diagnostics

The foundation of contemporary medicine is laboratory testing. They offer vital information for disease diagnosis, health monitoring, and treatment planning, from genetic sequencing to blood panels. However, manual errors, delayed results, and the difficulty of analysing big information are common problems with standard lab diagnostics. AI is transforming this field, transforming labs into fast and precise engines.

1. **Accuracy and Automation**: Routine laboratory procedures including sample sorting, analysis, and reporting are automated by AI-driven systems. *This guarantees consistency across thousands of tests every day and lowers human error.* For example, AI algorithms are significantly faster and more accurate than traditional methods at identifying aberrant cell morphologies in cancer screens or anomalies in blood smears.
2. **Identifying Patterns in Complicated Data**: Massive volumes of data, including proteome profiles, metabolomic fingerprints, and genomic sequences, are produced in modern labs. *AI is particularly good at finding correlations and patterns in these datasets that a person could never find by hand.* These insights make it possible to identify uncommon disorders, detect diseases early, and customize treatment regimens.
3. **Predictive Diagnostics:** Beyond analysis, AI can forecast the likelihood of a disease before symptoms manifest. *AI models can identify people who are at high risk of diabetes, cardiovascular disease, or autoimmune disorders by comparing lab findings to past patient data.* This enables medical professionals to take preventative action.
4. **Quickness and Effectiveness:** AI drastically shortens the

time it takes to get lab results. *Every minute matters in critical care situations like sepsis identification.* Real-time results processing and interpretation by AI-powered laboratories guarantees prompt healthcare decisions that save lives.

5. **Clinical Decision Support Integration:** AI in the lab doesn't function in a vacuum. It can effectively bridge the gap between raw data and patient care by offering clinicians relevant insights when linked with hospital systems. *These insights may include recommendations for next steps, possible drug interactions, or more tests.*

AI is changing laboratory diagnostics from reactive testing to proactive, predictive healthcare by improving accuracy, efficiency, and the capacity to take action before illness worsens.

Clinicians now have access to deeper and faster insights thanks to an automated, data-driven method that used to require laborious human labour.

5.4. Predictive Diagnostics: The Prospects for Prevention

In the past, medicine has been reactive: doctors treat patients after symptoms manifest. This paradigm is being reversed by AI-powered predictive diagnoses, which makes it possible to avoid illness before it manifests:

1. **Predicting Illness before Symptoms:** To find early warning signals of illness, AI systems examine enormous databases, including genetics, lifestyle factors, lab results, and medical histories. Subtle patterns in imaging scans or blood indicators, for instance, can reveal the early stages of cancer, diabetes, or cardiovascular disease far before traditional methods would. This makes it possible to make treatments at a time when treatment is much less invasive and much more effective.

2. **Customized Risk Assessments**: Each person has a different health risk. By combining many data points, such as environmental exposure and family history, AI can produce customized forecasts. Precision prevention replaces the one-size-fits-all approach to healthcare by providing patients with individualized suggestions for food, exercise, tests, or preventative therapies.

3. **Lives Are Saved by Early Intervention**: Predictive diagnostics' power lies not only in anticipation but also in action. Early lifestyle modifications, focused monitoring, and preventative treatments that lower the risk of serious illness are made possible by identifying high-risk patients. Early identification can significantly improve survival rates

in diseases like cancer, making potentially lethal situations treatable.

4. **Systems of Continuous Learning**: Over time, AI systems get better. They improve their predictive models as they process more data, making them more precise and perceptive of minute patterns. Because of this ongoing learning, predictive diagnostics will advance in tandem with medical knowledge, offering patients and physicians ever-more-accurate counsel.

5. **From Data to Decisions**: The most effective use of predictive diagnostics occurs when it is smoothly incorporated into clinical procedures. AI guarantees that insights are useful rather than merely educational by warning physicians about new hazards and recommending evidence-based treatments. This lowers hospital stays, medical expenses, and the burden of chronic illness by changing patient care from reactive treatment to proactive health management.

Predictive diagnostics is essentially a paradigm shift in medicine: it is now about anticipating, preventing, and enabling patients and physicians to take action before disease takes hold rather than just healing illness. Predictive, accurate, and preventative healthcare is the way of the future.

5.5. The Multimodal Diagnostics When AI Integrates Everything

Medical diagnosis has frequently been disjointed. In order to piece together a conclusion from fragmentary viewpoints, a clinician may examine lab reports, imaging scans, and patient history independently. This is altered by AI-powered multi-modal diagnostics, which unlocks previously unheard-of accuracy and insight by combining many medical data sources into a single, cohesive study:

1. **Combining Various Data Types:** Imaging scans, lab tests, genetic profiles, wearable device data, and even environmental and lifestyle factors can all be analysed simultaneously by AI. This comprehensive approach enables the emergence of minor associations, such as connecting genetic markers to abnormal imaging results or lab aberrations that would be undetectable when taken into consideration separately.
2. **Enhanced Diagnostic Precision:** AI lowers diagnostic uncertainty and errors by integrating several modalities. In cancer, for example, AI may combine pathology reports, MRI scans, and molecular profiling to differentiate benign growths from malignant tumours, ensuring that patients receive the appropriate treatment at the appropriate time. Multi-modal AI in cardiology can more precisely predict the risk of heart failure than any single test by correlating ECG patterns with blood biomarkers and images.
3. **Making Complicated Decisions Faster**: In real time, multi-modal diagnostics distils large, complicated datasets into useful insights. Clinicians make quicker, safer, and more confident decisions when they are informed about potential diseases as well as the level of risk and suggested next steps.
4. **The Pinnacle of Personalized Medicine**: Personalized

medicine is elevated by this method. AI gives individualized insights by combining all aspects of a patient's health data, including monitoring illness development, optimizing treatment plans, and even forecasting therapy responses.

5. **Diagnostic Synergy's Future:** A new era of completely data-driven, networked, and intelligent medicine is represented by multi-modal diagnostics. Clinicians can now make judgments based on a complete, 360-degree picture of a patient's health rather than being constrained by isolated tests or human processing power. Diagnostics are now a continuous, well-informed understanding of the human body rather than a collection of snapshots because to this convergence of information.

To put it briefly, multi-modal AI diagnostics is the pinnacle of medical intelligence, fusing technology, data, and expertise to provide more rapid, precise, and individualized healthcare than ever before.

5.6. Biases, Errors, and Dangers in AI Diagnostics

AI is not perfect, even as it provides previously unheard-of diagnostic skills. For AI systems to be used safely and effectively in healthcare, it is essential to comprehend the risks, mistakes, and biases they include.

1. **Representativeness and Quality of Data:** The quality of AI algorithms depends on the quality of the data used to train them. AI predictions may be erroneous or biased if training datasets are out-of-date, incomplete, or biased toward particular demographics. An AI system educated primarily on data from one ethnic group, for instance, can perform poorly for patients from different backgrounds, resulting in incorrect diagnosis or unfair treatment.

2. **Errors in Algorithms**: AI is prone to misinterpreting patterns, especially in unusual or edge circumstances. A deep learning algorithm may completely miss a modest indication of illness or misidentify a benign abnormality as cancer. AI lacks intuition and the capacity to think beyond its instruction, unlike human doctors, which could lead to grave mistakes if left unchecked.

3. **An over dependence on AI:** Clinicians run the risk of becoming overly reliant on AI advice, which would discourage critical thinking and second viewpoints. Blind faith in AI can exacerbate errors rather than prevent them, particularly in complicated situations.

4. **Explainability and Transparency**: Deep learning networks in particular function as "black boxes," making

predictions without presenting obvious justifications. Clinical and ethical issues are raised by this opacity, which makes it challenging for physicians to confirm findings, contest mistakes, or comprehend the logic behind recommendations.

5. **Legal and Ethical Consequences**: When AI makes mistakes, it raises the question of who is responsible. The AI developer, the doctor, or the hospital? If biases in AI are not addressed, they can worsen health disparities and create systemic injustices.

6. **Risk Mitigation**: Strict validation on a variety of datasets, ongoing AI performance monitoring, human supervision, and the incorporation of explainable AI (XAI) techniques that make decision-making more transparent are all effective defences. To guarantee that AI serves all patients in a safe and equitable manner, ethical standards and regulatory frameworks are also crucial.

In conclusion, AI diagnostics are tools, not infallible authority, even if they can significantly improve accuracy and efficiency. To guarantee that AI promotes better, safer, and more equitable healthcare outcomes, it is crucial to identify and resolve risks, mistakes, and biases.

5.7. The Ideal Diagnostic Team: AI + Physician

AI and human physicians working together will determine the direction of diagnostics in the future. AI offers speed, accuracy, and the capacity to find minute patterns in enormous amounts of data. Clinical judgment, contextual awareness, and the human touch necessary for interpreting results and interacting with patients are all contributed by doctors. When combined, they create a diagnostic team that is much more powerful than the sum of its parts:

1. **Increasing Human Knowledge:** Thousands of patient records, scans, and test results can be processed by AI in a matter of seconds, revealing abnormalities and offering potential diagnoses. This enables physicians to concentrate on areas where human skill is vital, such as sophisticated decision-making, uncommon cases, and nuanced patient care.
2. **Cutting Down on Mistakes and Missed Diagnoses:** Even the most skilled doctors sometimes miss minor symptoms or uncommon illnesses. AI sees things that humans might overlook, acting as a second pair of eyes. Research has demonstrated that combining physician judgment with AI recommendations greatly increases diagnostic accuracy.
3. **Instantaneous Decision Assistance:** AI may offer immediate feedback, highlighting critical results, forecasting the course of a condition, and making therapy recommendations based on the most recent scientific data. Physicians can then make quicker, more informed judgments by validating and contextualizing these recommendations.
4. **Learning Together:** The collaboration is mutually beneficial. Clinicians can educate AI systems through feedback, refining their accuracy, while AI exposes clinicians to new patterns,

rare instances, and emerging trends that could otherwise go missed. Both human knowledge and computer intelligence are improved by this ongoing learning loop.

5. **Preserving the Human Touch:** Even while AI is very good at computation and pattern recognition, it cannot take the place of empathy, communication, or the subtle judgment needed to explain complicated diagnoses and treatment options to patients. AI improves care without degrading it thanks to human control.

AI and doctors are essentially complementary to one another: doctors offer judgment, context, and compassion, while AI offers accuracy, scalability, and speed. This collaboration ushers in a new era of healthcare where errors are reduced, insights are maximized, and patients gain from the best of both worlds by transforming diagnostics from a human-alone project or a machine-alone procedure into a coordinated, intelligent, and patient-centered approach.

5.8. The Future: Self-governing Diagnostic Agents

The development of AI in healthcare suggests a daring new direction: self-governing diagnostic agents. Unlike traditional AI tools that help clinicians, these agents have the capacity to independently collect data, assess patient information, and produce early diagnoses—operating almost like a completely automated physician:

1. **Autonomous Diagnostic Agents: What Are They?**

   AI systems that can integrate multi-modal data—from wearable sensors, imaging scans, lab results, electronic health records, and patient-reported information—without continual human input are known as autonomous diagnostic agents. They are able to monitor patients continually, identify new health problems, and even make real-time action recommendations.

1. **Constant, Real-Time Health Tracking**:

   Autonomous agents are able to continuously monitor health, in contrast to sporadic doctor visits. AI receives data directly from wearables and connected devices, allowing for the early identification of abnormalities like arrhythmias, blood sugar increases, or mild cognitive deterioration. These systems provide a proactive, as opposed to reactive, approach to healthcare by spotting problems before they become more serious.

1. **Quickening Diagnosis in Distant or Overworked Environments**:

Autonomous diagnostic agents could offer expert-level evaluations in areas with limited access to physicians. These agents could be used by hospitals with large patient loads to eliminate diagnostic bottlenecks, prioritize urgent cases, and triage patients.

1. **Improving Medical Precision**:

To provide hyper-personalized diagnoses and treatment suggestions, autonomous agents can use genetics, lifestyle, environmental exposures, and past health data. This could enable highly customized early treatments, pharmaceutical regimens, or preventive actions based on each patient's particular profile.

1. **Difficulties Moral Issues:**

Important and questions are raised by autonomous diagnostics:

- *If an AI agent makes a mistake, who is responsible?*
- *When choices are made without human review, how can transparency and trust be guaranteed?*

When AI regularly analyses sensitive personal health data, privacy and data security also become critical. Deploying these systems properly will require careful regulatory frameworks, ethical standards, and human-in-the-loop oversight.

1. **A Look toward the Future**:

> Instead of taking the place of physicians, autonomous diagnostic agents aim to increase human potential by serving as watchful, constant collaborators in patient care. Imagine a period where healthcare becomes predictive, preventive, and personalized on a never-before-seen scale, where diseases are identified hours or days ahead of time, and where rural areas have real-time access to professional diagnostics.

In brief, autonomous diagnostic agents offer the next frontier of medicine, combining continuous monitoring, data integration, and predictive intelligence to revolutionize how we comprehend, identify, and respond to disease.

Conclusion: The Era of Intelligent Medicine

The incorporation of AI into healthcare signals a significant revolution in how diseases are discovered, diagnosed, and treated. AI has gradually advanced medicine toward accuracy, speed, and customization from the early days of guesswork to the current state of sophisticated pattern recognition. *Healthcare has moved from reactive care to proactive management thanks to medical imaging, laboratory tests, predictive models, and multi-modal AI systems.* AI is now a powerful collaborator for doctors, reducing errors, revealing hidden patterns, and enabling previously unthinkable customized interventions.

Yet, this transformation is not without challenges. Risks, biases, and ethical dilemmas remind us that AI is a tool, not a replacement for human judgment. *The future belongs to systems where* ***AI and Doctors,*** *combining computational intelligence with empathy, reasoning, and ethical oversight.*

Looking ahead, *autonomous diagnostic agents promise a healthcare ecosystem that is continuously aware, predictive, and adaptive—where diseases can be intercepted before symptoms appear, and care is delivered with unmatched precision.*

The horizon is clear: *medicine is entering an era where intelligence—both human and artificial—guides every decision, every diagnosis, and every treatment.*

The transition from guessing to AI-powered intelligence demonstrates that healthcare will not only be smarter in the future but also safer, quicker, and far more individualized. The doctor is still crucial, but because to AI, they are now a member of a diagnostic team that can produce results that were previously unthinkable.

With the advent of intelligent medicine, the possibilities are endless.

Chapter 6: AI in Therapy: Algorithm-Driven Therapies and Precision Medicine

Overview

A *diagnosis* reveals the problem.

What happens next is determined by *treatment.*

Standardized treatment protocols—guidelines developed from large population averages—have been the foundation of medicine for decades. However, no two people have the same biology, genetics, way of life, surroundings, or reaction to treatment.

AI is now changing medical care from a "one-size-fits-all" strategy to one that is customized, predictive, flexible, and constantly improved.

This chapter examines how AI is changing clinical decision-making, chronic disease management, medication discovery, therapy selection, and surgery.

6.1. The Transition from Precision Therapy to Generic Medicine

A "one-size-fits-all" approach to medical care was used for decades; individuals with the same condition were given the same medications, dosages, and treatment schedules. Although this general model performed rather well, it frequently failed to take into consideration the profound biological variations across people, including genetics, lifestyle, environment, metabolism, and even physiological changes that occur in real time.

The shift from generic medicine to actual precision therapy is now being propelled by AI.

AI systems are now able to recognize each patient's distinct biological signature by integrating genetics, biomarkers, imaging, wearable sensor data, and electronic health records. Clinicians can treat your specific form of the illness rather than treating the disease as a whole.

Important changes include:

- **From Standardized Treatment Plans To Customized Regimens:**

AI adjusts the types, timing, and dosage of medications according to the particular profiles of each patient.

- **From Reactive Medicine To Predictive And Preventative Therapy:**

Algorithms can anticipate treatment failure, complications, and disease progression before they happen.

- **From Population Averages → To Real-Time**

Personalization:

Therapies that adapt dynamically to the patient's changing state are made possible by continuous data from wearables and sensors.

- **From Trial-And-Error Approach To Data-Driven Accuracy:**

AI rapidly determines which treatments are most likely to be effective for each patient, minimizing side effects and treatment delays.

AI essentially turns treatment into a precision-guided, adaptable, and customized healing process in which medications are intelligently created for each individual rather than being generic.

6.2. AI in Customized Therapy Scheduling

AI is changing the way treatment plans are developed, moving away from standard clinical recommendations and toward highly customized therapeutic blueprints based on the biology, behaviour, and risk profile of each patient. Modern treatment planning incorporates real-time insights from AI systems that can analyse large, complicated medical datasets, rather than depending just on physician judgment and past data.

How AI Creates a Customized Treatment Strategy:

- **Comprehensive Patient Profiling:** AI creates a comprehensive, multifaceted patient profile by integrating genomes, medical imaging, lab results, lifestyle data, and even social determinants of health.
- **Determining Which Therapy Is Best for Each Person**: In order to suggest the therapy with the best chance of success for that particular patient, machine learning algorithms analyse millions of treatment-outcome patterns.
- **Dynamic and Adaptive Modification**: AI makes it possible to create living treatment plans that automatically update as new data becomes available, which is essential for patients with cancer, chronic illnesses, or intensive care units.
- **Prediction of Risk and Side Effects**: Clinicians can proactively modify the strategy before issues develop since AI can predict adverse medication reactions, complications, or resistance to therapy.
- **Accurate Drug and Dosage Selection**: Systems use individual metabolism, organ function, and genetic diversity to select the ideal medicine, dosage, and delivery schedule.
- **"Digital Twins" And Treatment Simulation**: By creating

patient-specific virtual models, or "digital twins," that mimic the effects of various treatments, advanced AI assists medical professionals in selecting the safest and most efficient course of action.

Real World Examples

- **Oncology:** Based on tumour genetics, AI systems like IBM Watson and Tempus match cancer patients with customized treatment regimens.
- **Cardiology:** For individuals who are not responding to conventional treatment, predictive models determine the optimal mix of antihypertensive.
- **Diabetes:** AI-powered devices, such as closed-loop insulin pumps, modify insulin dosage minute by minute to accommodate each person's unique glucose dynamics.

The Result

Better survival rates, fewer problems, lower treatment costs, quicker recovery times, and a more accurate, patient-centered approach are all results of AI-driven tailored therapy planning.

To put it briefly, AI turns treatment planning from a generic road map into a personalized, intelligent, and constantly changing healing plan created for every individual patient.

6.3. Drug Dosing Enhanced by AI: The End of Trial and Error

Conventional medication dosage frequently depends on clinician practice, weight-based computations, or demographic averages. Although this "trial-and-error" method works well for many, it might result in under dosing, overdose, side effects, or delayed therapeutic effectiveness, particularly in complex illnesses like cancer, heart disease, or critical care.

Drug dosing is being revolutionized by AI since it allows for accuracy, customization, and real-time modification.

AI-Enhanced Drug Dosing's Main Features:

- **Patient-Specific Modelling**: AI determines the best medication and dosage for each patient by analysing genetics, age, organ function, metabolism, and comorbidities. Pharmacogenomics data, for instance, can forecast a patient's drug metabolism, lowering the possibility of toxicity.
- **Constant Observation and Adaptation**: AI models get real-time physiological data from wearables and connected devices, enabling dynamic dose adjustments. AI-powered insulin pumps for diabetes automatically adjust dosage according to glucose patterns.
- **Predictive Safety Inspections**: Clinicians are informed of possible hazards by machine learning algorithms that predict negative reactions or interactions before they happen.
- **Treatment Outcome Simulation**: AI makes safer, quicker decisions by predicting how various dosage regimens would impact efficacy and side effects using digital twins or virtual patient models.

Practical Examples

- **Oncology**: AI models customize chemotherapy regimens to minimize toxicity and enhance tumour kill.
- **Critical Care:** Accurate physiological objectives are maintained by AI-driven dosage of sedatives or vasoactive medications in intensive care units.
- **Cardiology:** Tailored anticoagulant dosage prevents clot formation and lowers bleeding risks.

The Effect

- **Fewer Adverse Events:** Lowers hospital stays brought on by adverse medication reactions.
- **Quicker Therapeutic Response**: Patients attain therapeutic medication levels faster.
- **Reduced Costs:** Prevents problems and needless therapy modifications.
- **Precision Healthcare Recognized:** Every patient is given the appropriate medication at the appropriate time and dose.

AI essentially puts an end to the era of medicine dosage guesswork by substituting data-driven precision and real-time personalization, making medication delivery a science of exactitude rather than chance.

Chapter 7: AI in Patient Monitoring: Ongoing Care in a Networked World

Overview

Patient monitoring was episodic throughout the most of medical history. Only when they were ill did patients go to clinics. Physicians depended on snapshots: a daily glucose test, a blood pressure check every few months, and only in-hospital heart monitoring.

Conventional patient monitoring frequently depends on sporadic examinations, regular vital sign readings, and sporadic hospital stays. By providing continuous, real-time observation of patients' health state both in-hospital and remotely through linked devices, wearables, and smart sensors, AI-driven patient monitoring revolutionizes this strategy. Proactive intervention, quicker reaction to important events, and highly individualized treatment are all made possible by this change.

As important as the development of the stethoscope, *AI is transforming episodic care into continuous, real-time, predictive care.*

These days, health data is continuously sent by wearables, biosensors, smart implants, and digital biomarkers. These signals are quickly interpreted by AI, which may identify anomalous patterns long before symptoms manifest. This chapter examines how ongoing monitoring lowers hospitalization rates, averts medical crises, and gives people the power to take charge of their own health.

7.1. The Development of IoT-Enabled and Wearable Monitoring

Contemporary wearables, including patches, implantable sensors, and smart watches, continuously gather data on important health metrics like:

Blood pressure and oxygen saturation; blood glucose levels; heart rate and rhythm; respiratory patterns and activity levels.

Case Analysis

In 2024, Mount Sinai Health System adopted AI-enabled wearable monitors for post-cardiac surgery patients. The method recognized early indicators of arrhythmia in several patients before symptoms occurred, allowing physicians to intervene and avert hospital readmissions.

By sending this data to AI systems, patterns that are not obvious to the human eye are found, giving early alerts for potentially fatal situations.

7.2. Early Warning and Predictive Alerts

AI is quite good at spotting little departures from typical patterns. Algorithms can:

- Forecast heart failure exacerbations;
- Identify early respiratory failure in COVID-19 or COPD patients; and
- Predict sepsis hours before onset.

As an illustration, a UK hospital installed an AI predictive alarm system in its intensive care unit. In 72% of cases, the system was able to detect deterioration within six months ahead of routine monitoring, enabling life-saving action.

Instead of using raw data streams, these technologies give clinicians relevant insights and lessen the need for recurring inspection.

7.3. Remote Patient Monitoring (RPM): Care Outside of Hospital Enclosures

Patient monitoring at home or in remote locations is made possible by AI-enabled RPM, which lowers hospital visits while preserving patient safety:

- Ongoing vital sign monitoring using linked devices.
- Clinicians receive automated alert creation.
- Integration of telemedicine for online consultations

Case Study:

AI-powered glucose monitors were installed in a Canadian diabetic clinic. Clinicians were informed of abnormal readings by the system, which also continuously modified insulin recommendations. Within the first year, this led to a 40% decrease in emergency room admissions for hypoglycaemia or hyperglycaemia.

RPM lessens the strain on hospitals by promoting aging-in-place and democratizing access to healthcare.

7.4. Tailored Health Information

AI is revolutionizing the delivery of health information by converting general medical recommendations into highly customized insights. AI systems generate patient-specific risk assessments and dynamic health insights by synthesizing data from many sources, including wearable devices, electronic health records (EHRs), genetic profiles, imaging data, and real-time lab findings, in place of one-size-fits-all advice. This degree of customization enables medical professionals to foresee issues before they occur and provide patients with practical advice that takes into account their particular physiology, habits, and medical background.

Three main pillars are usually present in AI-driven customized health information:

- **Dynamic Medication's Modification**

Conventional drug schedules are fixed and frequently only modified at recurring clinician appointments. AI substitutes continuous, real-time drug optimization for this episodic approach.

AI systems can update prescription regimens by:

- Examining wearable data in real time, including oxygen saturation, heart rate variability, glucose levels, sleep patterns, and physical activity.
- Comparing test findings to identify changes in biomarkers that point to a deteriorating illness or adverse drug reactions.
- Using pharmacogenomics data to identify drug-drug and drug-gene interactions.
- Forecasting the patient's response trajectory and modifying

timing or dosage before unfavourable outcomes arise.

For instance, an AI model that automatically modifies insulin dosage recommendations based on food intake patterns, sleep quality, and stress physiology helps a diabetic patient wearing a continuous glucose monitor (CGM) avoid hypo- or hyperglycaemia and reduce glucose fluctuation.

- **Personalized Lifestyle Advice**

Lifestyle counselling becomes a precision science thanks to AI. AI makes recommendations based on real behaviour patterns, physiological reactions, and individual risk estimates rather than general advice like "exercise more."

Among these insights are:

- Tailored dietary recommendations based on metabolic trends, glucose reactions to particular foods, and micro biome data.
- Exercise plans based on musculoskeletal risk, recuperation time, and cardiovascular capacity.
- Sleep optimization techniques based on ambient sensor data, circadian rhythm analysis, and sleep stage deficiencies.
- Stress management measures that are initiated when autonomic imbalance or stress indicators are detected in real time.

As an illustration, an AI health coach might use smart watch data to identify elevated heart rate and irregular sleep patterns, combine it with growing inflammatory markers from blood tests, and suggest certain actions, such as earlier sleep schedules, less caffeine, guided meditation, or dietary adjustments.

- **Customized Treatment Schedules**

AI creates dynamic, changing treatment plans that adjust to the patient's changing state by integrating multidimensional patient data.

Predictive analytics that forecast future illness progression are used to refine personalized treatment options:

- Digital twins, which are virtual patient models used to evaluate the efficacy of various treatments.
- Risk stratification, which determines each biological profile's optimal treatment.
- Monitoring results and modifying treatment according on the patient's response.

These strategies combine clinical recommendations.

By combining professional recommendations with actual patient behaviour, these plans make sure that therapies are still applicable and efficient.

For instance, an AI system may use a patient's weight, blood pressure, and thoracic impedance readings to identify early indicators of fluid retention in the treatment of heart failure. Then, before hospitalization is required, it suggests making preventative changes, such changing the dosage of a diuretic or setting up an urgent examination.

AI can create patient-specific risk assessments by combining data from various sources, including wearables, EHRs, and lab results:

- Modifications to dynamic medications;

- Tailored lifestyle suggestions;
- Tailored treatment plans.

For instance, continuous blood pressure, weight, and activity data were examined by an AI platform for patients with heart failure. It reduced hospitalizations by over 30% and prevented bouts of fluid overload by automatically recommending changes to diuretics.

In Summary, Healthcare becomes proactive rather than reactive thanks to AI-powered personalized health information. AI guarantees that every facet of medical care—medication, lifestyle, and treatment approaches—is specifically tailored to each patient through ongoing data integration and customized modelling. This increases patient empowerment, participation, and long-term health stability in addition to improving outcomes.

7.5. Clinical Workflow Integration

AI-powered monitoring systems must be smoothly integrated into current healthcare workflows in order to reach their full potential. This entails incorporating AI in a way that improves rather than interferes with the way doctors engage with hospital systems, electronic health records (EHRs), diagnostic platforms, and communication tools. Effective integration guarantees that AI insights are incorporated into routine care, enhancing decision-making, cutting down on delays, and facilitating seamless information transfer between various clinical settings.

Effective clinical workflow integration is defined by two key elements:

7.5.1. A Seamless Transition Between Inpatient and Outpatient Treatment

Today's healthcare system is disjointed. Patients frequently lose important information when they travel between clinics, ERs, and hospital wards. By providing ongoing, cross-setting visibility of the patient's health status, AI-enabled technologies close these gaps.

- By automatically syncing patient data from wearables, home monitoring devices, and outpatient visits into the hospital's EHR as soon as a patient is admitted, artificial intelligence (AI) enhances continuity of care.
- Giving medical professionals access to current trends, such as declining vital signs, non-adherence patterns, or early warning risk ratings.
- Making preventive interventions possible, such as identifying a patient who is at high risk of hospitalization days before

clinical symptoms get worse.

- Developing unified care plans that track patients regardless of whether they are visited by a hospital team, specialist, or primary care physician.

For instance, the hospital system may send out alerts if a patient with heart failure exhibits modest indicators of decompensation at home, such as an increase in resting heart rate or a decline in activity. Clinicians may obtain a timeline of deterioration as soon as individuals arrive at the emergency room, allowing for more rapid and focused therapy.

The conventional information "black box" that frequently occurs between outpatient and inpatient care is eliminated as a result.

7.5.2. Data Visualizations for Easy Understanding

Massive amounts of data are produced by AI systems, far more than any therapist could possibly analyse by hand. Transforming this complexity into understandable, intuitive representations that facilitate quick, well-informed judgments is essential to effective integration.

AI improves clinical understanding through:

- Combining ongoing streams of lab results, wearable data, imaging results, and vital signs into user-friendly dashboards.
- Offering Heatmaps, risk curves, and trend lines that quickly demonstrate decline or improvement.
- Drawing attention to abnormalities or early warning indicators, such as abrupt changes in heart rate or an increased

risk of infection.
- Providing drill-down views, which allow medical professionals to quickly review the underlying data that underlies an alarm.

Particularly in hectic settings like intensive care units or emergency rooms, these representations lessen cognitive strain, expedite the diagnosis process, and guarantee that crucial information is never overlooked.

For instance, an ICU doctor can watch a single AI-generated dashboard that summarizes a patient's risk of sepsis, changes in organ function, and anticipated response to therapy—all updated in real time—instead of scrolling through thousands of EHR pages.

Integration with hospital systems and electronic health records (EHRs) is crucial for AI monitoring to be successful:

- A smooth transition between outpatient and inpatient care;
- Data visualizations for simple comprehension;
- Alerts ranked according to clinical significance

For instance, the ICU process at Johns Hopkins Hospital incorporates AI-driven monitoring. By providing real-time dashboards with predictive risk scores, nurses were able to respond to crucial events faster and improve patient outcomes.

AI monitoring is transformed from a stand-alone tool into a potent ally within healthcare systems through clinical workflow integration. AI becomes a logical addition to the clinician's workflow by facilitating smooth transitions between care settings and displaying data through user-friendly visuals. This guarantees safer, quicker, and better-coordinated patient care in addition to increasing efficiency.

7.6. Security, Privacy, and Ethical Issues

Massive amounts of extremely sensitive personal health data, from biometric measurements and physiological signals to daily routines and behavioural patterns, are produced by AI-driven continuous monitoring. Personalized care and strong predictive models are made possible by these databases, but they also bring with them important ethical obligations. To preserve trust and avoid harm, it is essential to make sure that patient information is used in a safe, equitable, and transparent manner.

The ethical environment of AI-enabled monitoring is defined by three crucial areas:

7.6.1. Ensuring HIPAA/GDPR Security Standards Compliance, Transparency, and Patient Consent

Strong patient data protection is the cornerstone of ethical AI monitoring. Patients need to be completely aware of how their data is used, who has access to it, and what security measures are in place because data gathering is ongoing, sometimes around the clock.

Important requirements consist of:

- **Explicit, Informed Consent**: Patients must understand when monitoring is taking place, what information is being gathered, and why.
- **Transparent Data Practices:** Organizations should provide clear explanations of data usage, storage, retention times, and deletion guidelines.
- **Compliance with HIPAA and GDPR**:
    - In the United States, HIPAA mandates stringent

  controls on patient data access, encryption, and sharing.
  - In the EU, GDPR requires data reduction, portability, and the opportunity for patients to seek erasure.
- **Secure Data Architecture:**
  - To stop data breaches, intrusion detection systems, multi-factor authentication, and end-to-end encryption are crucial.
  - Security against unwanted access: Role-based permissions guarantee that the patient's data can only be viewed by the appropriate professionals.
  - Security frameworks need to grow with the expansion of monitoring, from wearables at home to ICU equipment.

7.6.2. **Preventing Forecasting Models' Algorithmic Bias**

AI models use past data to learn. Incomplete, imbalanced, or biased data could lead to distorted outcomes from the model, endangering patient safety and increasing health inequities:

- To prevent over fitting to particular demographic groupings, it is important to use diverse training datasets.
- Frequent fairness tests and bias audits are carried out to find inadvertent discrimination.
- Transparent model creation that records known hazards, constraints, and training sources.
- Clinician supervision, making sure that AI forecasts complement professional judgment rather than take its place.
- Constant recalibration in response to fresh data, which keeps out-of-date trends from affecting treatment.

For instance, an AI model that was mostly trained on Western populations may underestimate cardiovascular risk in Asian or African populations. For healthcare to be equal, these gaps must be filled.

7.6.3. Monitoring Patient Autonomy and Intervention Frequency

If continuous monitoring is not properly controlled, it might easily veer toward over-surveillance. Even well-meaning notifications have the potential to become invasive, diminish patients' feeling of autonomy, or induce fear:

- **Respect for Patient Autonomy:** Patients must decide what information is gathered and have the option to refuse unnecessary monitoring in order for ethical implementation to take place.
- **Balanced alert mechanisms**: Systems should refrain from sending out too many notifications, which can overwhelm medical professionals or upset patients—a condition known as alert fatigue.
- **Clearly Defined Intervention Thresholds**: To prevent needless escalation, AI forecasts should only initiate action when absolutely essential.
- **Adaptive Monitoring Modes**: High-risk patients might need real-time alerts, while low-risk patients might need routine scans.
- **Human-Centered Design:** Instead of making patients feel like they are being monitored, evaluated, or micromanaged by algorithms, monitoring should empower them.

Clinical efficacy and patient dignity are both protected by ethical AI.

In conclusion, security, privacy, and ethics are structural foundations that decide whether AI improves healthcare or unintentionally undermines it; they are not optional elements of AI-enabled monitoring. Building trust and attaining appropriate AI integration in contemporary healthcare require data protection, justice, and respect for patient autonomy.

7.7. AI's Effect on Patient Monitoring

The way healthcare systems detect, understand, and react to patient health is being radically changed by AI-driven monitoring. AI makes it possible to move toward predictive, proactive, and highly responsive care rather than waiting for catastrophes or worsening symptoms. This ushers in a new era when hazards are foreseen rather than merely handled after the fact, redefining patient monitoring at every level from home-based wellness tracking to critical care unit surveillance.

The impact of AI causes a number of significant shifts in healthcare practice:

7.7.1. **Transitioning to Predictive Intervention from Reactive Care**

Clinicians are not notified by traditional monitoring until anomalies manifest.

By evaluating constant data streams, spotting minute patterns that are imperceptible to human observation, and predicting decline before clinical symptoms appear, AI replaces this reactive paradigm:

- Sepsis can be detected hours in advance by predictive algorithms.
- Days before hospitalization is required, AI algorithms can detect early indicators of heart failure decompensation.
- AI powered by wearables can identify respiratory deterioration or arrhythmias in real time, triggering an early medical examination.

In the end, this preventive strategy saves lives by lowering complications and avoiding ICU admissions.

7.7.2. **Ongoing, Contextualized Health Monitoring**

AI uses data from wearables, smart medical devices, EHRs, imaging results, lab tests, environmental sensors, and patient behaviour and lifestyle aspects to monitor patients holistically.

As a result, a dynamic, changing health profile is created that is updated with each heartbeat, step, sleep cycle, and lab result. AI gives medical professionals ongoing context, such as what preceded a decline, what risk factors are present, and what trajectory the patient is likely to follow, in contrast to conventional single-point measures.

7.7.3. Improved Precision and Decreased Human Error

By eliminating subjective vital sign interpretation, reducing missed early warning indicators, filtering noise from massive data quantities, and prioritizing clinically significant patterns, artificial intelligence (AI) standardizes monitoring.

This increases monitoring's sensitivity and specificity, guaranteeing that important changes cause alerts while lowering false alarms. Clinicians can concentrate on meaningful intervention instead of data sorting since they obtain clearer, more trustworthy information.

7.7.4. Using Self-Monitoring to Empower Patients

AI-powered technologies allow for monitoring outside of hospital boundaries. Mobile health apps, remote monitors, smart inhalers, blood pressure sensors, continuous glucose monitors, and AI-powered coaching systems are all ways that patients can take an active role in their own care.

These solutions give patients early warning notifications, medication reminders, tailored health scores, and immediate feedback. As a result, patients are more empowered, health-conscious, and actively involved in managing and preventing illness.

7.7.5. Enhanced Clinical Effectiveness and Workload Reduction

Many laborious aspects of monitoring are automated by AI:

Data analysis, trend identification, alert prioritizing, critical change documentation, and risk stratification

Instead of raw data, clinicians receive succinct, actionable insights. This significantly lowers cognitive strain, speeds up response times, and frees up staff members to focus more on patient-centered duties.

For instance, an AI system might alert only the 3% of data that shows actual clinical risk rather than manually examining 24-hour vital signs.

7.7.6. Improved Results via Prompt Interventions

Interventions that are:

- Earlier;
- More focused;
- Less intrusive; and
- More successful in averting problems are made possible by

predictive monitoring.

AI enables care to be provided at the appropriate time—before deterioration becomes severe—whether it is through prescription adjustments, urgent review scheduling, or the activation of fast response teams.

Conclusion

Artificial intelligence is transforming patient monitoring into a highly predictive, intelligent, and continuous system that foresees issues rather than responding to them. It improves clinical accuracy, increases patient participation, simplifies processes, and produces better results. Monitoring has evolved from simple observation to early intervention, prevention, and large-scale tailored care in this predictive era.

AI in patient monitoring is a paradigm change for the medical field. AI converts episodic therapy into ongoing healing by continuously monitoring, evaluating, and forecasting patient health. In the future, patients will be seamlessly monitored in community, hospital, and home settings, resulting in a totally connected healthcare environment.

Chapter 8: The Path Ahead: Using AI to Create Robust Healthcare Systems

Overview

The sophistication of hospital architecture and the genius of AI algorithms won't be the only factors defining the future of healthcare. Resilience is a significant concept that will shape it. A resilient healthcare system is one that adjusts, reorganizes, and cares for patients even in the face of unforeseen changes in the outside environment. These future-ready systems are beginning to rely on artificial intelligence as its engine and glue. AI is turning health services from brittle structures into adaptive ecosystems, from predicting disease outbreaks to facilitating continuity of care during emergencies.

Using actual worldwide examples and experience-based case studies that demonstrate how AI is already preparing systems for the uncertainties ahead, this chapter examines how AI will improve healthcare resilience.

8.1. Introduction: Shock Redefines the World

In addition to being a health disaster, the COVID-19 pandemic demonstrated the fragility of many health systems. Hospitals are full. Supplies are running out. Patients with chronic conditions are cut off from care. Governments are rushing to gather information. Infrastructures for telemedicine were put into operation overnight.

The world witnessed the fallout from decades of inadequate investment in adaptability.

Resilience emerged as the new benchmark in the aftermath.

Nations started to wonder:

- *How can we predict the next crisis?*
- *How can millions of patients be guaranteed continuity?*
- *How might we lessen our reliance on human-only procedures?*
- *How can care be expanded in the event of a breakdown in physical access?*

AI provides responses to all of these queries.

And in reality, not just in theory.

8.2. AI as the Foundation of Resilience after Pandemics

Future historians will probably refer to 2020–2030 as the "decade of AI-enabled healthcare transformation." Why?

Because nations came to the crucial realization that AI is not an add-on in the years that followed the outbreak. Infrastructure is what it is.

It serves as the basis for health systems' ability to:

- Predict dangers;
- Automate routine tasks;
- Redistribute limited resources;
- Provide care remotely; and
- Continually learn from data.

Case Study: AI-Powered Resilience Model in South Korea

Following the 2015 MERS outbreak, South Korea developed a real-time AI epidemic surveillance system. This technique detected infection clusters prior to official notifications during COVID-19:

- The deployment of mobile test stations was led;
- ICU bed allocation was optimized; and
- Contact tracing was expedited.

Because of this, South Korea was able to prevent lockdowns across the country and continue to provide vital medical services even during periods of high demand.

This is an example of resilience.

AI enhances human skill rather than replaces it, offering clarity in the midst of chaos.

8.3. Systems for Predictive Health: Seeing the Future before It Happens

Foresight is the first step toward true resilience. AI is quite good at identifying patterns and signals that human planners cannot see.

Forecasting Epidemics

Current AI models examine:

- Hospital admissions,
- social media signals,
- mobility data,
- wastewater virus loads,
- Vector patterns and climate.

They find epidemics weeks or days ahead of conventional surveillance.

Example: BlueDot - The business that witnessed COVID Arriving

Nine days before to the WHO alert, in December 2019, BlueDot, a Canadian AI company, identified a cluster of pneumonia-like infections in Wuhan.

AI is not alarmed.

AI doesn't make assumptions.

AI just recognizes patterns.

Predicting Hospital Increases

In the past, hospitals planned staffing and beds based on historical norms. These days, AI forecasts ICU bed needs with remarkable accuracy using:

- Machine learning demand models;
- Real-time admissions;
- Emergency call trends; and

- Flu season projections.

Case Study: AI ICU Predictor in New York City

During COVID-19's deadliest days, hospitals in New York employed AI to:

- Forecast Shortages Of Oxygen.
- Identify impending patient waves, and
- Reassign ventilators throughout the city.

By reallocating resources before shortages occurred, this predictive intelligence prevented thousands of deaths.

Early-Warning Systems for Supply Chains

AI currently monitors hundreds of factors in international medical supply chains, such as production trends, weather interruptions, and shipping delays, and notifies governments of vulnerabilities.

This implies that the globe won't be caught off guard by the next crisis.

8.4. Continuous Care in a Disrupted World: AI Assistants, Telehealth, and Remote Monitoring

Millions of people learned throughout the pandemic that healthcare could be provided anywhere, not just in clinics. AI made telemedicine a whole ecosystem of ongoing treatment that doesn't depend on a patient's physical location.

Never-Sleeping Remote Patient Monitoring (RPM)

AI algorithms that identify irregular cardiac rhythms, respiratory decline, glucose abnormalities, and early indicators of heart failure get continuous streams of data from wearables and home medical equipment.

Case Study: Preventing Readmissions for Heart Failure

AI monitoring was used to 1,000 heart failure patients in a US study. Early intervention was made possible by the system's average detection of deterioration five days prior to symptoms.

Readmissions to hospitals decreased by 30%.

Delivered concurrently are continuity, resilience, and personalization.

Telehealth in Remote and Remote Areas

Telemedicine is no longer an experiment in many African countries. It is now the foundation of care.

AI chatbots, for instance, pre-screen patients and guide them to the appropriate care level in Kenya and Uganda. This lowers travel expenses and frees up scarce clinical personnel to concentrate on complicated situations.

Clinical Assistants with AI: The Digital Workforce

These days, AI assistants may summarize medical histories, generate consultation notes, assess lab results, make differential diagnosis recommendations, and remotely monitor patients.

These mechanisms preserve stability in times of crisis, when human capacity declines.

8.5. Independent Healthcare Operations: Self-Managing Hospitals

Operations are just as important to a robust healthcare system as clinical treatment. Hospitals are becoming self-optimizing ecosystems thanks to AI.

Intelligent Medical Facilities

The cutting-edge Ng Teng Fong General Hospital in Singapore employs AI to:

- Control bed flow;
- Plan procedures;
- Maximize energy use;
- Monitor equipment;
- Automate medication distribution; and
- Direct robot porters.

As a result, resource waste decreased and emergency wait times dramatically decreased.

Case Study: Predictive Operations Command Centre at Cleveland Clinic

An AI-powered "Mission Control Room" was constructed by the Cleveland Clinic to:

- Foresee bottlenecks;
- Monitor admissions citywide;
- Optimize patient transfers; and
- Deploy staff in real time.

This system maintains the stability of the entire healthcare ecosystem, much like an airport control tower.

Digital Twins: Future Simulation

Hospitals or entire health systems can use digital twins to test staffing scenarios, assess emergency response plans, model pandemics, and optimize layout and flow.

The creation of a national digital twin for Saudi Arabia's healthcare system is a first for the globe and will have a lasting impact on global health planning.

8.6. Population-Level Resilience: Using AI to Prepare the Nation

A resilient country has the most intelligent health infrastructure rather than the greatest number of hospitals.

Platforms for National Digital Health

AI is used by nations like Estonia, Rwanda, and the United Arab Emirates to study population illness trends, immunization gaps, risk factors, regional health disparities, and emergency response requirements on unified health data systems.

Health ministries can detect risk long before populations experience symptoms thanks to these tools.

Climate and Disease Forecasts

AI forecasts how climate change will fuel:

- Malnutrition caused by agricultural failure;
- Cholera outbreaks;
- Heat stroke risk; and
- The spread of malaria.

Example: Brazil's Dengue Prediction Engine

Cities can send out fumigation teams ahead of time thanks to Brazil's AI dengue system, which forecasts mosquito population rises weeks in advance.

In certain states, dengue hospitalizations have decreased by more than 40% thanks to our prediction model.

8.7. AI Governance, Ethics, and Trust Adaptability

Great monitoring is necessary when there is a lot of power. For systems to rely on AI in times of crisis, it must be reliable. Algorithmic fairness, explainability, data protection, and accountability are important factors to take into mind.

Case Study: The Predictive Risk Scandal in the Netherlands

Thousands of innocent families were unjustly identified by an AI benefit fraud detection system. The ensuing political fallout served as a global warning about the dangers of unbridled AI.

Such mistakes are unaffordable in the healthcare industry.

Transparency is necessary for resilience, particularly in automated systems.

8.8. The Healthcare Workforce Prepared for AI

Technology is only as powerful as its users. Clinical intuition, data literacy, AI navigation abilities, and digital empathy are all necessary for the future healthcare workforce.

Case Example: The AI Training Initiative at the Mayo Clinic

Clinicians must complete AI literacy training at the Mayo Clinic to make sure they comprehend how AI functions, how to challenge AI recommendations, and how to incorporate AI into patient interactions.

Patient trust has increased and AI healthcare technologies have been adopted more easily as a result of this training.

8.9. Global Equity: The Ethical Need for Robust AI

If a system leaves millions behind, it cannot be said to be resilient. AI presents previously unheard-of chances to reduce disparities in healthcare around the world.

Examples of AI-Driven Equity include:

- AI translation tools for multilingual consultations throughout India;
- Drone delivery of medications in Ghana and Rwanda;
- Diagnostics using smartphones in remote locations without laboratories;
- Artificial intelligence (AI) ultrasound technologies that let nurses do scans without radiologists;
- Remote cancer patients can receive virtual oncology consultations.

Case Study: The SmartCare EMR System in Zambia

One of the most sophisticated national electronic medical record systems in Africa was invented by Zambia.

What is it?

Zambia's national electronic medical record (EMR/EHR) platform, SmartCare, was created by the Ministry of Health in collaboration with foreign partners. SmartCare Pro, a standardized national EHR that facilitates interoperability (FHIR/HL7/JSON/XML), lab integration, reporting, and commodity management across public facilities, was first created as a longitudinal, clinic-level patient record to support HIV care and maternal/child health.

Reach and Implementation.

In the late 2000s, SmartCare was chosen as the national system, and it has been gradually implemented at the provincial and facility levels. The Ministry of Health, SMART Zambia Institute, and implementing partners (CDC, CIDRZ, and others) have spearheaded implementation through training, local hosting, and sporadic SmartCare Pro platform upgrades. Recent initiatives include countrywide rollouts of digital literacy training for healthcare professionals and lab integrations.

Important advantages were noted.

- **Continuity of Care:** longitudinal records that are accessible across clinics enhance retention and follow-up, particularly for maternal-child and HIV/TB programs.
- **Program Monitoring and Reporting**: Partners utilize SmartCare's distinctive service delivery reporting and regular program data for planning and assessment.
- **Workflow Enhancements:** Real-time data entering speeds up decision-making (lab results, medication history) and minimizes duplicate registers when properly integrated.

Documented Common Difficulties

- **Infrastructure and Connectivity**: Uneven hardware availability, sporadic power, and constrained network bandwidth continue to be significant obstacles at many sites.
- **Human Resources and Training**: inconsistent usage of the EMR is caused by personnel turnover, varying digital literacy, and workload pressure; continuous training is necessary.
- **Data Quality and Workflow Fit**: staff acceptance and data completeness have been impacted by incomplete or delayed data entry, parallel paper procedures, and discrepancies between the system design and local workflows.
- **Sustainability and Governance**: finance, local ownership, and transparent data governance for research vs national reporting have required ongoing effort.

Evidence and Impact

In Zambia, empirical assessments and qualitative research demonstrate enhanced program data timeliness and favourable opinions when infrastructure and training were sufficient; however, they also frequently draw attention to implementation flaws that obscure potential benefits (data completeness, usability, and consistent use). Large-scale nationwide EMR rollouts in low-resource environments often have inconsistent outcomes.

Current Guidance and Scale-Up Learning.

1. **Iterative improvements (SmartCare → SmartCare Pro):** improved interoperability and analytics are supported by modular, standards-based updates (FHIR/HL7) and lab/LMIS connections.
2. **Invest In People And Infrastructure:** as crucial as software features are training, local IT support, dependable power and connectivity, and streamlined point-of-care workflows.
3. **Data Governance and Use:** provide feedback loops and explicit governance to help physicians understand the importance of high-quality data (dashboards, clinical decision support).
4. **Partner Coordination:** Sustaining upgrading and analytical capabilities is made possible by coordinated donor/partner support (CDC, CIDRZ, SMART Zambia Institute).

Diagram: The SmartCare EMR System Architecture

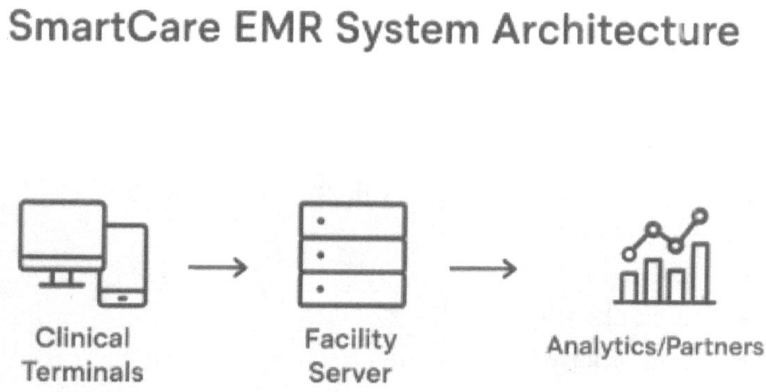

Figure 8: The SmartCare EMR System Architecture

SmartCare may soon be able to forecast:

- Risks of maternal complications;
- Adherence to HIV treatment; and
- Regional medicine shortages thanks to AI integration.

The development of SmartCare in Zambia demonstrates both the potential and the labour-intensive nature of national EMR systems in low-resource environments: national EMRs can significantly enhance continuity of care and program monitoring when they are in line with clinical workflows, supported by infrastructure and training, and upgraded toward open standards.

However, long-term impact depends more on sustained investments in connectivity, local capacity, governance, and ongoing iterative co-design with frontline users than on features.

Africa is now leapfrogging rather than catching up.

8.10. The Future Healthcare System: From Homes to Hospitals

The primary point of care will shift to the home by 2035.

Home-based Diagnostics

AI-powered portable gadgets will enable citizens to:

- ECGs,
- Blood chemistry tests,
- Lung function assessments,
- Early cancer marker monitoring, and
- Automated interpretations.

Individual AI Health Protectors

Each person might have a personal AI that constantly evaluates:

- Biometrics,
- Lifestyle,
- Genetics,
- Environment, and
- Problems early indicators long before illness manifests.

A World in Which Healthcare Is Ubiquitous

AI transforms society as a whole into a care setting rather than hospitals:

- Homes,
- Offices,
- Schools, and
- Public places.

Distribution, not concentration, is the source of resilience.

8.11. Conclusion: 2035's AI-Resilient Healthcare System

The nature of health systems will change over the next ten years.

Systems that:

- Foresee dangers instead of reacting to them;
- Automate stability instead of relying only on humans;
- Disperse care instead of centralizing it;
- Continuously learn instead of staying static will be the most successful;
- Rather than favouring a select few, defend all citizens equally.

AI is the design of the healthcare system of the future, not just a technology advancement.

Resilience won't be a choice in 2035.

In the face of emerging pandemics, climate shocks, population pressures, and economic changes, it will be the crucial factor that decides whether societies prosper or fail.

And AI will be at the core, acting as a silent protector that strengthens each layer of the system rather than as a cold machine.

Chapter 9: Prospects for the Future of AI in Healthcare

Overview: The Future of Medical Intelligence

The field of healthcare is about to enter a new era where intelligence is not limited to humans. In medical practice, AI is changing from a tool to a collaborator, partner, and co-creator. Future developments in AI in healthcare promise previously unheard-of opportunities to transform patient care, treatments, diagnostics, and even the medical system itself.

This chapter examines cutting-edge applications, new trends, and the revolutionary possibilities of AI in the upcoming 10 years.

Healthcare is about to enter a revolutionary period in which artificial intelligence (AI) will become a fundamental component of medical systems, influencing patient engagement, workforce planning, diagnosis, treatment, and medication research. The next ten years will redefine what is possible in medicine as foundational models, real-time biosensors, autonomous clinical systems, and AI-driven decision engines come together.

In Chapter 9, the future directions of AI in healthcare are examined, along with the trends, technologies, possibilities, and risks that will shape the field's future.

9.1. Beyond Precision Care: Ultra-Personalized Medicine

Beyond precision care, ultra-personalized medicine is the next significant advancement. Ultra-personalized medicine uses a comprehensive and constantly updated picture of each patient's particular biology, behaviour, environment, and lifestyle to customize treatment in real time, whereas precision medicine groups individuals based on shared genetic or clinical features.

This method incorporates:

- AI-driven predictive models;
- Real-time data from wearables and sensors;
- Genomics, proteomics, and metabolomics;
- Digital twins—virtual copies of specific patients;
- Individual psychological and social components.

As a result, patients receive care that is dynamic—medications that self-adjust, treatment regimens that change in response to physiological changes, and therapies tailored to the individual biology of each patient rather than population-level averages.

Ultra-personalized medicine shifts the focus of treatment from "what works for most people" to "what works for this person, at this moment." It is the epitome of human-centered, accurate, and responsive healthcare.

The next advancement in personalization goes well beyond the methods used in precision medicine today.

9.1.1. Medical Twin Technology

A digital twin is an entirely digital copy of a patient's physiological systems that is updated on a regular basis using wearable sensors, biomarkers, imaging, and genetics.

Future features include:

- Creating "virtual clinical trials" that drastically cut down on R&D time;
- Predicting disease onset weeks or months before symptoms appear; and
- Predicting how a patient will react to various treatment plans before administering therapy;

9.1.2. Case Study: Heart Failure Digital Twin

Digital cardiac twins that can nearly perfectly forecast arrhythmias and optimize pacemaker settings have been tested by Siemens Healthineers and the University of Sheffield.

9.2. Ambient Intelligence - Hospitals That Think

Hospital settings that are equipped with networked sensors, artificial intelligence (AI) systems, and smart gadgets that continually monitor, assess, and react to staff and patient needs—often without direct human input—are referred to as ambient intelligence. These "thinking hospitals" function as intelligent ecosystems where technology is used sparingly yet its advantages are always present.

Smart patient rooms that monitor vital signs, detect falls, adjust lighting, and maximize sleep without invasive equipment are among the key features:

- AI-assisted workflow automation, in which computers anticipate patient decline, provide critical alarms to the appropriate physicians, and plan activities such as transportation, medicine delivery, or room assignment.
- Context-aware settings that can recognize patterns of behaviour, such as whether a patient is walking, resting, or in distress, and react accordingly.
- Integrated safety systems that track equipment, monitor hand hygiene, flag environmental hazards, and identify infection risks.
- Hospitals become proactive, responsive, and self-optimizing settings thanks to ambient intelligence. It increases patient safety, boosts clinical effectiveness, and facilitates more individualized, seamless treatment, turning the hospital into a silent healing partner.

Ambient AI, or intelligent technologies integrated into beds, walls, cameras, IV pumps, and clinical areas, will be a feature of hospitals in the future.

9.2.1. Never-Sleeping Sensors

Hospitals will use completely integrated sensor networks to measure staff exhaustion, medication adherence, patient falls with no false alarms, early sepsis patterns, and silent patient deterioration.

Wards will become proactive health environments instead of reactive ones thanks to AI systems.

9.2.2. AI in the Smart ICU Case Study

Ambient sensors that monitor respiratory patterns from ceiling-mounted radars were installed in a Canadian intensive care unit. Compared to human clinicians, mortality-related worsening was identified up to six hours earlier.

9.3. Self-governing Medical Systems

AI is gradually moving from decision support to autonomous and semi-automated healthcare delivery.

9.3.1. Independent Diagnostics

Autonomous AI systems with regulatory approval will do the following tasks:

- Screening for diabetic retinopathy;
- Evaluating skin lesions;
- Interpreting chest x-rays; and
- Performing basic triage and risk rating.

These systems, which offer specialized accuracy with little infrastructure, will particularly revolutionize low-resource nations.

9.3.2. Independent Processes

Eventually, emerging robotic systems will be able to:

- Robotic endoscopic examinations;
- Autonomous venepuncture;
- Automated ultrasonography; and
- Precision microsurgeries.

9.3.3. Case Study: Autonomous Ultrasound for Maternal Care in Rural Areas

By enabling community health workers in Africa to conduct intricate ultrasound scans without the need for radiologists,

Butterfly Network's AI solutions are significantly boosting maternal outcomes.

9.4. AI + Robotics: The Automated Hospital's Ascent

The automated hospital—a medical setting where intelligent robots carry out basic, repetitive, and high-precision tasks while human physicians concentrate on sophisticated, high-touch care—is emerging more quickly because to the combination of AI and robotics.

While robotics offers the hands by carrying out activities quickly, accurately, and consistently, artificial intelligence (AI) provides the brains by evaluating data, forecasting needs, and organizing workflows.

Among the major developments are:

- Autonomous delivery robots that move supplies, food, specimens, and drugs between wards without the need for a human escort.
- AI-driven robotic surgical systems that provide previously unheard-of levels of accuracy, stability, and customized surgical planning.
- Automated sterilization and disinfection machines, which lower the risk of infection and enhance hospital hygiene.
- Rehab robots with AI capabilities that facilitate remote patient progress monitoring and personalized physical treatment.
- Intelligent inventory and logistics systems that minimize inefficiencies, replenish supplies, and monitor equipment.

Diagram: AI + Robotics: The Automated Hospital

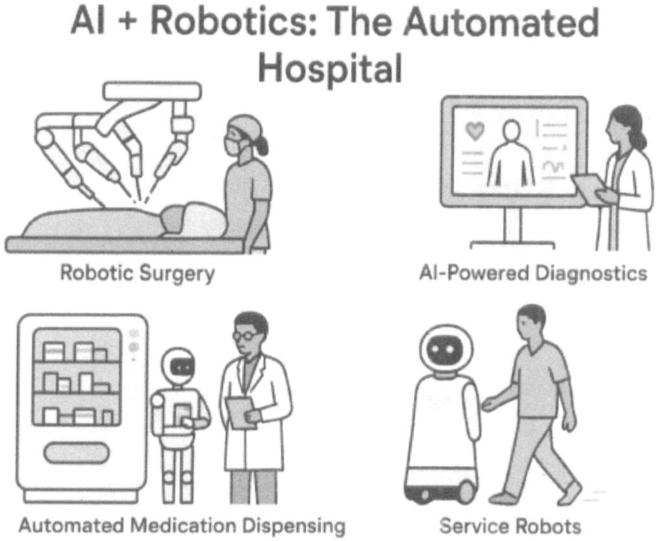

Figure 9: AI + Robotics: The Automated Hospital

Hospitals are becoming incredibly safe, predictable, and efficient thanks to AI and robots, where automation speeds up processes, lowers errors, and improves patient outcomes. This rise ushers in a new era in which hospitals function as intelligent, coordinated systems that can provide care at previously unheard-of levels of quality and scope.

Predictive, real-time AI will let hospitals fully integrate robotics.

9.4.1. Robots for Hospital Logistics

Robots with AI capabilities will manage inventory, move lab samples, dispense pharmaceuticals, and disinfect.

Error rates and the burden of nurses will decrease as a result.

9.4.2. Reasoning engines in surgical robotics

Surgical robots of the future will comprise:

- Real-time anatomical mapping;
- Autonomous tissue tracking;
- In-procedure decision engines; and
- Automatic mistake correction.

For instance, in controlled studies, the STAR robot performed autonomous soft-tissue surgery on pigs with more accuracy than human surgeons.

9.5. AI for Health Management at the Population Level

AI is enabling health systems to monitor, forecast, and control risks across entire populations, moving healthcare from hospital-centered treatment to community-level prevention. AI enables governments, insurance companies, and public health organizations to target high-risk populations, intervene earlier, and create more intelligent health policies rather than reacting to illness after it happens.

Important changes consist of:

- **Early Illness Identification at Scale**: AI examines data from clinics, pharmacies, wearables, and community health initiatives to uncover new trends, like an increase in flu cases, a surge in hypertension, or early diabetes hotspots.
- **Targeted Interventions**: Before problems worsen, high-risk persons can receive early notification, be connected to community health workers, or receive assistance through customized programs.
- **Resource Optimization:** By allocating personnel, ambulances, vaccines, and pharmaceuticals where they are most needed, predictive algorithms reduce waste and enhance service delivery.
- **Smart Public Health Planning:** AI assesses behavioural, environmental, and socioeconomic variables to identify vulnerabilities and direct long-term health initiatives.
- **Continuous, Real-World Monitoring**: Entire communities can be tracked for infectious disease outbreaks, maternity health, mental health trends, and chronic illness management using wearables, remote sensors, and smartphone apps.

The future health system will be proactive, preventive, and deeply ingrained in daily life as AI makes it possible for healthcare to reach outside hospital walls, improving outcomes for millions of patients at once rather than just one.

Healthcare will move from hospitals to the community thanks to AI.

9.5.1. Intelligence in Epidemiology

AI models in the future will monitor:

- Real-time disease outbreaks;
- Population stressors (climate, diet, air pollution);
- Health disparities among minorities; and genomic risk clusters.

AI will be used by governments to manage digital epidemiology dashboards for the security of the country's health.

9.5.2. Predictive Public Health

AI for predictive public health will predict:

- The burden of chronic illnesses;
- The requirement for future hospital capacity;
- Increases in mental health; and
- Seasonal disease spikes.

Micro-targeted public health initiatives are made possible by this.

9.6. The Super Clinician Era: AI-Augmented Human Clinicians

AI will improve doctors, not replace them.

9.6.1. Amplification of Intelligence

Support for doctors will come from:

- AI scribes,
- predictive analytics,
- Customized therapy calculators, and
- Genomic recommendations in real time.

There will be a new role in medicine: The AI-Enhanced Clinician received training in algorithmic thinking, risk modelling, and data science.

9.6.2. Evolution of Skills

Physicians will spend less time:

- Documenting;
- Doing information searches; and
- Carrying out repetitive activities.

And more time:

- Developing relationships with patients;
- Making decisions; and
- Handling difficult ethical situations.

9.7. Bio-AI Interfaces: Combining Algorithms and Biology

Bio-AI interfaces are the new frontier where artificial intelligence and biological systems work together harmoniously to create significant new opportunities for human augmentation, diagnosis, and treatment. These interfaces enable AI to interact directly with, impact, and learn from live systems in real time rather than only processing biological data.

Important advancements include:

- AI-integrated neural interfaces, in which brain–computer interfaces (BCIs) convert neural signals into digital commands, allowing for early cognitive monitoring, communication for paralyzed patients, and movement restoration;
- Smart biosensors that continuously monitor molecular signals (such as hormones and immune markers) and use AI to instantly interpret changes.
- Closed-loop therapeutic systems that automatically modify treatment in response to feedback from the body, such as AI-controlled insulin pumps, neurostimulators, or cardiac devices.
- Living bio-hybrid machines, which combine biological tissue with robotic control for improved adaptability and healing;
- AI-guided synthetic biology, where algorithms create new enzymes, vaccines, or cell therapies with previously unheard-of precision.

Fundamentally, Bio-AI interfaces erase the lines between digital and biological, creating opportunities for real-time biological intelligence, self-adjusting therapies, and improved human capacities.

This convergence ushers in a time when biology and algorithms develop—and heal—side by side, taking medicine beyond monitoring.

The nexus of biotechnology and artificial intelligence is the next frontier.

9.7.1. Intelligent Implants

AI models will be integrated into implants that:

- Identify anomalies;
- Automatically modify medication administration; and
- Interact in real time with medical professionals.

AI-powered insulin implants, pacemakers that anticipate arrhythmias, and neuro-modulation devices for epilepsy and depression are a few examples.

9.7.2. AI-Brain Interfaces

This includes:

- AI-interpreted brain impulses;
- Neural implants that restore motor function.
- Research on cognitive enhancement; thought-to-speech devices for individuals with paralysis.

AI might be able to accurately decode internal speech in 15 years, helping those who are unable to communicate.

9.8. The Acceleration Era of AI-Driven Drug Discovery

Drug development is becoming a fast, accurate, and highly predictive discipline thanks to artificial intelligence (AI). By analysing complicated biological data, predicting molecular interactions, and identifying interesting compounds long before laboratory testing starts, artificial intelligence (AI) speeds up the 10–15 years and billions of dollars that traditional drug development typically takes.

Important developments consist of:

- **Predictive Molecule Design**: AI systems reduce trial-and-error experimentation by producing innovative molecules with high probabilities of efficacy and minimal toxicity.
- **Virtual Screening at Scale**: Top prospects can be found more quickly than with traditional methods by evaluating millions of possible drug candidates in silico.
- **Clinical Trial Optimization**: AI increases trial efficiency and success rates by choosing the best patient populations, forecasting responses, and tracking results in real time.
- **Repurposing Current Medications**: AI finds novel therapeutic applications for licensed pharmaceuticals, reducing development expenses and time.
- **Integration with Omics Data**: To find new targets and gain a thorough understanding of disease mechanisms, genomic, proteomic, and metabolomic datasets are studied.

Diagram: AI-Driven Drug Discovery Pipeline

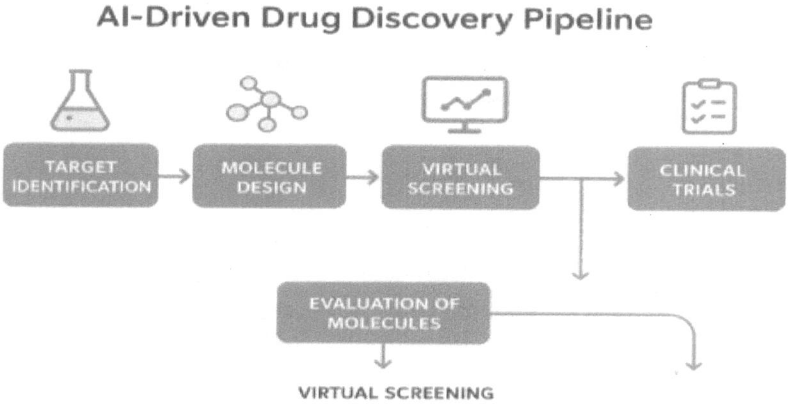

Figure 10: AI-Driven Drug Discovery Pipeline

As a result, the drug pipeline is significantly accelerated, allowing previously incurable illnesses to become viable targets, life-saving treatments to reach patients more quickly, and development costs to decline. In this day and age, drug discovery is no more a reactive process but rather one fuelled by predictive, artificial intelligence.

The 12-year drug discovery lifetime will be reduced to two to three years.

9.8.1. Models of Molecular Foundations

Future AI will create organ-on-a-chip simulations, create whole new chemicals, predict toxicity with almost perfect accuracy, and design customized treatments.

9.8.2. Clinical Trials Using AI First

Clinical studies will get smaller, shorter, more focused, and more predictable.

Case Example: By forecasting 200 million protein structures, DeepMind's AlphaFold revolutionized drug research and development by facilitating quicker drug target identification worldwide.

9.9. Human, Legal, and Ethical Risks Up ahead

Risks increase as capacities do.

9.9.1. **Dangers of Algorithmic Autonomy**

- *When an autonomous system misdiagnoses, who is in charge?*
- *How can judgments made by opaque models be verified?*

9.9.2. Scale Bias

Large-scale systems in the future may:

- Increase prejudice;
- Discriminate against minority groups;
- Misinterpret data from underrepresented communities.

9.9.3. Risks to Infrastructure and Security

AI-targeted cyberattacks on hospitals, altered diagnostic results, genomic data theft, and attacks on autonomous clinical machines are some of the risks.

9.9.4. **Moral Conflicts**

- Human dignity vs automation;
- Privacy versus constant surveillance; and
- Efficiency versus compassion,

9.10. The 2040 AI-First Healthcare System

Healthcare is predicted to be AI-first by 2040, with AI serving as the primary coordinator of almost all aspects of treatment. According to this vision, AI systems would seamlessly integrate human experience with artificial intelligence to anticipate, diagnose, plan, and coordinate care in real time, in addition to helping physicians.

Important traits consist of:

- **Proactive And Predictive Care:** AI continuously monitors patients at the individual and population levels, anticipating illness before symptoms manifest and facilitating early therapies.
- **Ultra-Personalized Care:** Each patient receives care that is dynamically adapted to their surroundings, lifestyle, physiology, and genetics, changing as their disease does.
- **Autonomous Hospital Operations:** Routine chores are managed by robotics, intelligent logistics, and AI-driven clinical processes, freeing up physicians to concentrate on high-level decision-making and patient contact.
- **Integrated Population and Community Health:** AI connects clinics, hospitals, and community health networks to provide care wherever patients reside and prevent disease on a large scale.
- **Ethical, Secure, And Transparent Systems:** Strict privacy, security, and bias-mitigation guidelines govern how AI functions, guaranteeing patient autonomy, equity, and confidence.
- **Continuous Learning:** Every patient interaction, intervention, and outcome feeds back into AI models, speeding up medical innovation and knowledge throughout

the system.

As a result, healthcare will be ubiquitously intelligent, highly tailored, and seamlessly predictive in 2040. While physicians use AI as a co-pilot, allowing them to concentrate on the human aspect of treatment, patients benefit from shorter hospital stays, improved chronic disease management, and more proactive wellness advice. The system is now completely integrated, anticipatory, and adaptable rather than reactive.

An AI-first health ecosystem of the future will consist of:

9.10.1. Constant, Instantaneous Health

Patients will be kept under observation at home using:

- Bio patches driven by AI;
- Smart toilets;
- Ambient sensors; and
- Predictive health dashboard.

Hospitals will not be used for routine check-ups, but rather for acute, specialized care.

9.10.2. Completely Independent Care Routes

From the symptom to the remedy:

1. AI prioritization.
2. AI diagnostics.
3. Suggestions for AI therapy.
4. A robotic process.
5. Monitoring AI recovery.

Selective supervision and intervention will be provided by human therapists.

9.10.3. **Equity in Global Health**

AI will close gaps for underserved groups, low-resource countries, and rural places. Autonomous, reasonably priced solutions will democratize care at the specialist level.

9.11. Conclusion: A Revolution in Healthcare Underway

AI in healthcare is not about replacing doctors; rather, it is about creating a world in which hospitals become intelligent ecosystems that heal before harm occurs, where no patient experiences avoidable disease, and where treatment is safer, quicker, and more individualized.

AI will be the most significant medical development in human history. The trend is evident: *medicine is moving from human-limited to intelligence-augmented, from generalist to individualized, and from reactive to predictive.*

In 2040 and beyond, the healthcare systems that are ready for these paths now will be at the forefront.

Table of Figures

Bibliography

1. *Alowais SA, Alghamdi SS, Alsuhebany N, Alqahtani T, Alshaya AI, Almohareb SN, et al. (September 2023). "Revolutionizing healthcare: the role of artificial intelligence in clinical practice"[1]. BMC Medical Education.* ***23*** *(1) 689. doi[2]: 10.1186/s12909-023-04698-z[3]. PMC[4] 10517477[5]. PMID[6] 37740191[7].*

2. *Shmerling RH (March 27, 2024). "Can AI answer medical questions better than your doctor?"[8]. Harvard Health Publishing.*

3. *Hamet P, Tremblay J (April 2017). "Artificial intelligence in medicine". Metabolism. Insights Into the Future of Medicine: Technologies, Concepts, and Integration.* ***69S****: S36 – S40. doi[9]:10.1016/j.metabol.2017.01.011[10]. PMID[11] 28126242[12].*

4. *Pouke M, Häkkilä J (December 2013). "Elderly healthcare monitoring using an avatar-based 3D virtual environment"[13]. International Journal of Environmental Research and Public Health.* ***10*** *(12): 7283–7298.*

1. *https://www.ncbi.nlm.nih.gov/pmc/articles/PMC10517477*
2. *https://en.wikipedia.org/wiki/Doi_(identifier)*
3. *https://doi.org/10.1186%2Fs12909-023-04698-z*
4. *https://en.wikipedia.org/wiki/PMC_(identifier)*
5. *https://www.ncbi.nlm.nih.gov/pmc/articles/PMC10517477*
6. *https://en.wikipedia.org/wiki/PMID_(identifier)*
7. *https://pubmed.ncbi.nlm.nih.gov/37740191*
8. *https://www.health.harvard.edu/blog/can-ai-answer-medical-questions-better-than-your-doctor-202403273028*
9. *https://en.wikipedia.org/wiki/Doi_(identifier)*
10. *https://doi.org/10.1016%2Fj.metabol.2017.01.011*
11. *https://en.wikipedia.org/wiki/PMID_(identifier)*
12. *https://pubmed.ncbi.nlm.nih.gov/28126242*
13. *https://www.ncbi.nlm.nih.gov/pmc/articles/PMC3881167*

doi[14]:10.3390/ijerph10127283[15]. PMC[16] 3881167[17]. PMID[18] 24351747[19]. S2CID[20] 18535954[21].

5. *Stokes F, Palmer A (October 2020). "Artificial Intelligence and Robotics in Nursing: Ethics of Caring as a Guide to Dividing Tasks Between AI and Humans". Nursing Philosophy.* **21** *(4) e12306. doi[22]:10.1111/nup.12306[23]. PMID[24] 32609420[25].*

6. *Krzhizhanovskaya VV, Lees MH, Dongarra JJ, Sloot PM (eds.). Computational Science – ICCS 2019. Lecture Notes in Computer Science. Vol. 11537. Cham: Springer International Publishing. pp. 633–645. doi[26]:10.1007/978-3-030-22741-8_45[27]. ISBN[28] 978-3-030-22741-8[29].*

7. *Zhao Y, Wood EP, Mirin N, Cook SH, Chunara R (October 2021). "Social Determinants in Machine Learning Cardiovascular Disease Prediction Models: A Systematic Review"[30]. American Journal of Preventive Medicine.* **61** *(4): 596–605. doi[31]:10.1016/j.amepre.2021.04.016[32]. PMID[33] 34544559[34].*

14. *https://en.wikipedia.org/wiki/Doi_(identifier)*
15. *https://doi.org/10.3390%2Fijerph10127283*
16. *https://en.wikipedia.org/wiki/PMC_(identifier)*
17. *https://www.ncbi.nlm.nih.gov/pmc/articles/PMC3881167*
18. *https://en.wikipedia.org/wiki/PMID_(identifier)*
19. *https://pubmed.ncbi.nlm.nih.gov/24351747*
20. *https://en.wikipedia.org/wiki/S2CID_(identifier)*
21. *https://api.semanticscholar.org/CorpusID:18535954*
22. *https://en.wikipedia.org/wiki/Doi_(identifier)*
23. *https://doi.org/10.1111%2Fnup.12306*
24. *https://en.wikipedia.org/wiki/PMID_(identifier)*
25. *https://pubmed.ncbi.nlm.nih.gov/32609420*
26. *https://en.wikipedia.org/wiki/Doi_(identifier)*
27. *https://doi.org/10.1007%2F978-3-030-22741-8_45*
28. *https://en.wikipedia.org/wiki/ISBN_(identifier)*
29. *https://en.wikipedia.org/wiki/Special:BookSources/978-3-030-22741-8*
30. *https://doi.org/10.1016%2Fj.amepre.2021.04.016*
31. *https://en.wikipedia.org/wiki/Doi_(identifier)*
32. *https://doi.org/10.1016%2Fj.amepre.2021.04.016*
33. *https://en.wikipedia.org/wiki/PMID_(identifier)*
34. *https://pubmed.ncbi.nlm.nih.gov/34544559*

8. *He B, Kwan AC, Cho JH, Yuan N, Pollick C, Shiota T, et al. (April 2023). "Blinded, randomized trial of sonographer versus AI cardiac function assessment"*[35]*. Nature.* ***616*** *(7957): 520–524. Bibcode*[36]*:2023Natur.616..520H*[37]*. doi*[38]*:10.1038/s41586-023-05947-3*[39]*.*

9. *Bax M, Thorpe J, Romanov V (December 2023). "The future of personalized cardiovascular medicine demands 3D and 4D printing, stem cells, and artificial intelligence"*[40]*. Frontiers in Sensors.* ***4*** *1294721. doi*[41]*:10.3389/fsens.2023.1294721*[42]*. ISSN*[43] *2673-5067*[44]*.*

10. *Han SS, Moon IJ, Lim W, Suh IS, Lee SY, Na JI, et al. (January 2020). "Keratinocytic Skin Cancer Detection on the Face Using Region-Based Convolutional Neural Network"*[45]*. JAMA Dermatology.* ***156*** *(1): 29–37. doi*[46]*:10.1001/jamadermatol.2019.3807*[47]*. PMC*[48] *6902187*[49]*. PMID*[50] *31799995*[51]*.*

11. *Aghamohammadi M, Madan M, Hong JK, Watson I (2019). "Predicting Heart Attack Through Explainable Artificial Intelligence"*[52]*. In Rodrigues JM, Cardoso PJ, Monteiro J, Lam R,*

---

35. *https://www.ncbi.nlm.nih.gov/pmc/articles/PMC10115627*

36. *https://en.wikipedia.org/wiki/Bibcode_(identifier)*

37. *https://ui.adsabs.harvard.edu/abs/2023Natur.616..520H*

38. *https://en.wikipedia.org/wiki/Doi_(identifier)*

39. *https://doi.org/10.1038%2Fs41586-023-05947-3*

40. *https://doi.org/10.3389%2Ffsens.2023.1294721*

41. *https://en.wikipedia.org/wiki/Doi_(identifier)*

42. *https://doi.org/10.3389%2Ffsens.2023.1294721*

43. *https://en.wikipedia.org/wiki/ISSN_(identifier)*

44. *https://search.worldcat.org/issn/2673-5067*

45. *https://www.ncbi.nlm.nih.gov/pmc/articles/PMC6902187*

46. *https://en.wikipedia.org/wiki/Doi_(identifier)*

47. *https://doi.org/10.1001%2Fjamadermatol.2019.3807*

48. *https://en.wikipedia.org/wiki/PMC_(identifier)*

49. *https://www.ncbi.nlm.nih.gov/pmc/articles/PMC6902187*

50. *https://en.wikipedia.org/wiki/PMID_(identifier)*

51. *https://pubmed.ncbi.nlm.nih.gov/31799995*

52. *https://link.springer.com/chapter/10.1007/978-3-030-22741-8_45*

Don't miss out!

Visit the website below and you can sign up to receive emails whenever Patrick Mukosha publishes a new book. There's no charge and no obligation.

https://books2read.com/r/B-A-HJNZ-MEEKI

BOOKS 2 READ

Connecting independent readers to independent writers.

Did you love *AI in Healthcare: The Doctor Will Code You Now*? Then you should read *AI in Law: Justice by Algorithm*[53] by Patrick Mukosha!

[54]

Discover how artificial intelligence is transforming the legal world in ***AI in Law: Justice by Algorithm*.**

Patrick Mukosha explores AI-driven legal research, contract analysis, predictive judgments, and courtroom innovations, showing how technology can **enhance efficiency, reduce bias, and expand access to justice**—all while preserving the **essential role of human judgment and ethics**.

Featuring global case studies from the U.S., China, Singapore, and Europe, this book is a must-read for legal professionals, students, policymakers, and anyone curious about the future of law.

---

53. https://books2read.com/u/bPBqRd

54. https://books2read.com/u/bPBqRd

Step into the era of "**Justice by Algorithm**" and see how humans and AI can collaborate to create a fairer, smarter legal system.

About the Author

Patrick Mukosha is an ICT & Management Consultant. With 15+ years of IT experience, he's passionate about all things ICT. He also loves to bring ICT down to a level that everyone can understand. His works have been quoted on Academia by Researchers and ICT Practitioners (www.academia.edu). He has a PHD and MBA from AIU, USA, BSc(Hons) ICT, UEA, UK, Dipl, CCT, UK. He's a founder of PatWest Technologies.

www.ingramcontent.com/pod-product-compliance
Lightning Source LLC
LaVergne TN
LVHW090316210926
848480LV00001B/269
* 9 7 9 8 2 3 2 8 4 8 8 8 0 *